UNFUCKWITHABLE

A Guide to Inspired Badassery

LINDSAY MANFREDI

Rose Gold Publishing, LLC

Unfuckwithable – A Guide to Inspired Badassery

Unfuckwithable

(adj.) when you're truly at peace and in touch with yourself, nothing anyone says or does bothers you, and no negativity or drama can touch you.

---The only book you need to get the fuck out of your own way.

For Bella and Hazel

Table of Contents

UNFUCKWITHABLE

A Guide to Inspired Badassery

LINDSAY MANFREDI

Un*fuck*withable

I bleed the blood of all who's lost
Keep searching no matter the cost
Backed in a corner, this maze of rot
It belongs to everyone

Chasing the Sun

I'd like for you to take a few moments with me to close your eyes and do a little daydreaming. If you think about it, when is the last time you had a daydreaming session? As adults, we rarely have time to do such 'childish' and 'time-wasting' exercises (so we think), so indulge me, please.

Imagine what's going on around you if you are doing the one thing you love to do. You're making a living doing this thing, you live in a state of pure bliss and joy, and you have a deep inner knowing that you were meant to be here at this specific moment, doing this particular thing. What does that feel like?

Now imagine the home you live in. What does it look like? Where is it located? How many bedrooms and bathrooms does it have? How is it decorated and what does it smell like? Imagine being in your bedroom first thing in the morning as you wake up and then go about your daily routine…what does that feel like in your daydream? Imagine walking through your day, having it play out EXACTLY as you desire, doing the things you love, and having a pure sense of gratitude and fulfillment. You are filled with nothing but joy and appreciation.

Now imagine that you have everything in life you could possibly desire; true love, abundant prosperity, loving relationships, and a sense of purpose. Hell, not even a "sense" of purpose, a fucking KNOWING that all is right in the world. How would you love to live THAT life? Well, that's what we're going to attempt to figure out in this book.

Now, before you stop here and think, "This bitch is crazy," let me give you a bit of my background because you've probably never even heard of me. Or perhaps you read my blog or listen to my music. Maybe you just picked this book up because the title was cool.

For those of you who don't know me, I play music in one of my all-time favorite rock bands and this is my first book. I've wanted to write a book for as far back as I can remember because I felt like I could contribute inspiration to other people. I've also been through a lot of bullshit in my life and have learned great lessons, and I'm still learning. While I've always had an idea of what that book would look like, this particular book turned out to be something completely different than what I originally had in mind.

Unfuckwithable came in the middle of a very spiritual yet chaotic place in my life. It came while I was going through a breakup. I was in the midst of leaving many people, whom I considered friends but who were not healthy for me, traveling to different places in the United States, working on an album of my dreams, and not having a home. I literally had to live the title and decide to BECOME unfuckwithable to get out of the place I was in emotionally and spiritually. I was letting way too many people's thoughts, opinions, and criticisms get the best of me. Yet, during all of this change and craziness, which I am still going through, I know it has been and will continue to be, okay. I know that where I am in my life right now is 100% part of the Universe's divine plan for me. This is true for you too, if you've picked up this book.

It's funny because the older I get, the calmer I've become in just being okay with things exactly as they are. I haven't always been like this. I've certainly always had a sense of calm about me, even in my wild days, but I would still have private meltdowns. And I still have insecurities. I'm not 100% where I want to be but I'm going on this journey of life just like everyone else, and I've accomplished a great deal in my forty-one years here. Maybe me not really giving tons of shits in my past is why I've been able to do the things I've done thus far. I don't know. What I do know is that I have some stories to share with you that have worked for me in my life, and I'm happy you're here.

Do you ever feel like you go and go and go and get nowhere? Like you're in some survival state of madness and the stress that you feel is like you've hit rock bottom? Or maybe you're not even at rock bottom, but the bottom is definitely coming out from underneath you and you have no control over it? I'll tell you; I've worked my ass off over the last 20 years and have had some great things happen, but I've hit bottom quite a few times. The only way to go is up, once you're there, so it's not a bad thing.

In all of these ups and downs, I've had people around me that I'd like to slap around a little bit because I wanted them to get their heads out of their own asses. There are so many people out there, around us every day, who are just locked into an unspiritual, egotistical, negative way of thinking and living, who have no clue how to tap into the power of their true Source, that creative Source which has made them. These people can be brilliant, creative, and kind but are lost in their ego and mostly get in their own way. I am hoping to inspire change in that regard, hence this book.

I'm not judging any of these people (okay, well, maybe a little)! I've just been there and done that. It wasn't until after reading a plethora of books, going to a million websites, and learning from truly inspiring people, about the Law of Attraction, that I was open to having an enlightened me. A me where my shit is finally getting straight (yet not ALL the way straight, as this whole spiritual/life journey is just that…a journey), and here I am, writing this book for you. If you want change in your life, then this book is for you. So, let's get to it.

ALL of the things I'm going to share with you matter: If you choose to practice the things you learn here as much as possible, I promise, it will change your life for the better.

I'll be honest, when I began this book, I had no idea what was going to show up in these pages. What I DID know was that it was coming from Spirit, so I didn't give a shit what anyone else thought about it. I also knew I was called to do this in such a way that it wouldn't stop pouring out.

My life has changed, incorporating these principles that I've learned. These things are now everyday habits in my life. These are the things I am asking you to not only consider but to make a daily practice on your road to being inspired AF.

All of us have habits and ways of thinking that have been ingrained within us from the time we were children. These are things we just kind of do without thinking, so let's chat about habits we'd like to change for a minute. We do things daily that are either good for us or bad for us. We have thoughts daily that are either good for us or bad for us. I'm assuming you've picked up this book because the title seemed a little intriguing and perhaps you care too much about what other people think of you. Maybe you want to change that. Perhaps there are many things you'd like to change and make better. But all this change takes place starting inside, and you probably don't know dick about changing your thoughts and changing your life, and you're probably sick and tired of being sick and tired. I know I was.

Becoming unfuckwithable begins with changing the negative ways you think and behave into positive thoughts and behaviors, one thing at a time, one day at a time. I'm going to share with you some information to change your life based on a handful of powerful daily activities. None of this is new information. It's just coming from me, in my own words, with my own story.

Are you ready to create these POSITIVE habits and thoughts versus the same ole', same ole' way of behaving and thinking? Are you prepared to dive into taking charge of your own destiny by changing your mind? I'm out to create a fundamental change in the way you think about things so you can SEE things differently.

Always keep this in mind; what you focus on expands. So often we get caught up in the world-fed drama of our daily environment rather than being aware of, or taking control of, our own mind and emotions. To be fully conscious of the way you process things and change them into thoughts that genuinely serve your life takes honesty, commitment, some balls, and a fucking lot of faith. It's about finding what you love to do and creating your life around that. It's about the tools you need to make positive habits so you can make a difference in your life and the lives around you. It's about making the Law of Attraction work in YOUR life. Let's DO this.

Oh, and one more thing: ***Fuck Your Excuses!***

Yeah, we all have them. We're all too busy, too tired, too overworked, too overstressed…fuck your excuses, because THOSE are what you shouldn't "have time" for. The bottom line is you're too busy getting in your own damn way. Now, take the time to get the fuck out of it. Remember, *YOU* are the most important person in your life.

Let me say that again…

YOU are THE most important person in your life.

- Not your husband/wife/partner/lover, if you so choose to have one or many.
- Not your child/children, if you so choose to have one or many.
- Not your boss, not your mother or father or siblings or friends.

An hour a day of making yourself unfuckwithable is the most important thing you can do, and there can be no excuses. You want change? I can only guess you put the "I need change" vibe out there somewhere in the Universe so let's assume that the answer is a resounding, "Fuck yes, I want change." Well then, prepare to be 100% responsible for doing the things you need to do in your life to make that possible. Now, let's DO this.

"For those who believe in God, most of the big questions are answered. But for those of us who can't readily accept the God formula, the big answers don't remain stone-written. We adjust to new conditions and discoveries. We are pliable. Love need not be a command nor faith a dictum. I am my own God. We are here to unlearn the teachings of the church, state, and our educational system. We are here to drink beer. We are here to kill war. We are here to laugh at the odds and live our lives so well that Death will tremble to take us." — *Charles Bukowski*

Basics AF - Love Yourself

1. Practice Loving Yourself (This Includes Your Body!)

When is the last time you took a look in the mirror and said, "I love you." to yourself? Think about it. If you don't remember, I'd like to give you a gentle reminder that the love you have for yourself is the most important thing in the Universe. I'm going to begin this whole journey with you by challenging you to go to the store, or your old desk drawers full of unused index cards or Post-It notes, and make some reminders to yourself. Here is what goes on those cards:

I love you.

I am beautiful.

I am unique.

I am the only me.

I am a child of perfect creation.

I am inspired.

I build empires.

I am vibrant.

I am perfectly imperfect and that's utterly, fucking perfect.

Look, I know this may seem cheesy, but I don't care. Carry these cards with you or place them in spots around your home to remind yourself that YOU are the only you. Every morning you wake up, look in the mirror, and remind yourself that you are a perfect creation and you are NOT a mistake. You're made of the same stuff this brilliant galaxy is made of. You are perfect. You HAVE TO START LOVING YOU if you want any of your dreams to come true. Learning to love and respect yourself is not only vital for you to make a change in your own life but also in making a difference in the lives of those around you.

I understand this isn't as easy as it may sound. You may be thinking, "How can I possibly love myself when I look like this?" or, "How can I love myself when I've made this mistake or that mistake?" Well, it all starts with a decision. Everything you do in life that creates change begins with the decision to make the change.

I've struggled with loving myself for years. I still struggle at times. It's easy given the advertisements we are consumed by and to look in the mirror and think, "If I could just lose these last however many pounds, if my belly were just a little tighter, if my nose was just a little smaller, if I were only a better Mother, if I only had better clothes, more money, blah, blah, blah ..." You get the point. If I continued to do that, I'd be a hermit in my house not going anywhere until I was an unrealistic version of myself. I'd be 'if-ing' my life away, and that's just not cool. I am super fucking special, and so are you. It doesn't matter what ANYONE ELSE says but it does matter what you say to yourself. Hell, until you learn to love yourself and cherish yourself, nothing in your life will change. Here's why: Your words and thoughts matter, and everything you say and think is your reality.

You CREATE your own reality. So many people live in such a state of unconsciousness that they don't understand the damage they're causing themselves by saying terrible things to themselves about themselves. It's FUCKED. I have gotten SO much better at this, but it's taken me years. Look, YOU are the creator here when it comes to loving yourself. So, while you or I may not be the best lover of thyself, I would suggest you fake it till you make it to get to your purpose. You tell yourself that you're beautiful, smart, strong, healthy, loving, creative, vibrant, (there are so many words here) and that you truly have all you need, then I promise, everything you desire will show up perfectly at the perfect time.

Going back decades, my first year attending a public school was when I was in the eighth grade. There was a boy in my science class who insisted on making me feel about as shitty as I could possibly feel on a daily basis. He said I was fat and called me "big nose" and "big lips." It was so bad that when I would smile in photos, I would bite my bottom lip in just a little bit to make it look like it wasn't so big. I have photos of me doing this. It's insane.

Luckily for me, as I was experiencing this bullying at school, one day I went home and started watching Oprah. Thank God for her show! It was one of those perfect life 'a-ha' moments. Looking back now, I feel like this was my first actual experience where the Universe was giving me a message. Oprah had a plastic surgeon as a guest on her show, along with women who were getting injections into their lips to make them more plump. This was the moment I stopped biting my lower lip. Shit, people were PAYING LOADS OF MONEY for something I had naturally. BOOM. My lips are fucking perfect. And so is my Italian/German nose. I don't give a shit anymore. However, I sometimes have to remind myself of that, if that makes sense.

For example, I remember when my band had a photoshoot for our new record and our promo stuff was about to be released into the world. Our photographer, Emily Tingley, who is a baller photographer, asked me to look to my right. I immediately said, "Ugh, I hate profile shots because of my nose." Why is it that, years after this false idea was put in my head, I still unconsciously went straight there? Conditioning? Perhaps. But this is why it's so important to love ourselves for who we are and remind ourselves daily that we are beautiful, unique, and perfect. That was an unconscious thought. I STILL took issue with my nose over something that happened twenty-five years ago. So I had to stop my thought in its tracks and say to myself, "My nose is fucking perfect." In place of those negative thoughts, I retrain my brain to think more positively about myself. Every day I continue to work on replacing those self-deprecating thoughts. The days of me obsessing over my nose are now few and far between. However, there are times when those thoughts come creeping in, like Freddy Krueger, just waiting to keep me in an egotistical nightmare.

The thing is, just like middle school, I wanted to fit in and I wanted a place to belong and for people to like and accept me. I don't think that will ever change. It's probably just human nature. I haven't necessarily wanted to fit into some kind of mold, but true acceptance is a thing. Looking back now, maybe I never really liked myself. I certainly didn't understand the concept of loving myself. I DO understand these things now.

I also understand that, way too often, we forget who we are. We forget how powerful we are. We forget how beautiful and unique we are. We forget that WE are the creators of our lives. We get so lost in the shit of every day. We get so lost in expectations, some from ourselves, some from others, but it's time to slow down and remember that we can only give love when we love ourselves. We get lost in our egos and trying to be model perfect with perfect bodies and thigh gaps and shit. It's so fucking ridiculous. Today, it's time to stop. It's time to regroup and find out WHO you are. That begins by loving yourself and finding out what you genuinely love to do and that you have the power to make shit happen. You are the only YOU. And thankfully, you're still alive because you're reading this. That means there's still time. At this moment.

If you want to change the physical appearance of your body, let's say, drop those extra pounds you've been holding onto, this takes constant daily actions. I'm not talking get model skinny. I'm talking about getting to a healthy you.

I used to be a personal trainer. Helping others get to a place of good health was something I was and still am passionate about. So I'd like to take a few moments to discuss this.

You have ONE body. You only get one chance this time around. Don't fuck around with it. Yes, you are beautiful no matter what size you are, but loving yourself means not letting yourself and your health go by the wayside.

I'm not a picture of perfect health. Since I've had a Twitter account, one of the things in my bio is that I'm "health nut – ISH." Not perfect by any means, but I do strive to keep myself looking ten years younger than I am. I smoke cigarettes sometimes, I smoke weed occasionally, I participate in recreational drugs at times, I drink wine and tequila. I live my life, but I do my best to balance everything out with meditation, yoga, working out, and "life" food. I personally follow Lyn-Genet Recitas' New York Times Bestselling books, *The Plan*, and *The Metabolism Plan*. She helps teach people to eat the foods that are chemically right for their own bodies. The principles in her books are pretty much my bible when it comes to my everyday eating and hydration. At the end of the day, it's so important to take care of one thing you can control: your decisions on how to treat and feed your body. If you are struggling with weight and eating in a manner that doesn't promote good health, I highly suggest picking up the books I just mentioned. It is not a diet; it's a lifestyle change that focuses on eating foods that are in chemical alliance with your body and keeping internal inflammation at bay, which has been found to basically cause all the diseases and fuckery in our bodies.

So many of the foods loaded with sodium and excess sugar are the easiest to grab when we convince ourselves we "don't have enough time to eat healthy or cook." These unhealthy choices can have severe impacts on our health. I know that when I eat processed foods regularly, I feel like complete shit. When I eat "life" food, I feel terrific. "Life" food includes food that comes from the Earth in the forms of fruits, vegetables, seeds, nuts, organic meats, and other foods low in sodium and sugar. I don't know about you, but I WANT to feel GOOD. I don't want to feel bad. Plus, I love to work out, and if I eat like shit, my workout is kind of shitty too. We have these fantastic bodies; let's treat them amazingly.

Also, we have to talk about hydration. I once heard on NPR that if you don't drink enough water, the cells in your body don't function in the way they should. I listened to this when I was eighteen so I've been on the water kick ever since. Water is part of the fountain of youth. I'm forty-one and still get carded everywhere I go. People always tell me I look younger than I am. I believe it's because I've kept myself adequately hydrated for twenty years. I even have an app on my phone called "Water Balance" to help me keep it in check. Proper hydration gives you more energy, makes you not eat as much, and helps you sleep better.

How much water should you drink? A rule of thumb to go by, which I learned from Lyn-Genet, is that whatever your weight is in pounds, you should divide that by two and drink that number in ounces of water. For every thirty minutes of exercise, add an additional eight ounces. And if you drink alcohol, the number of ounces of alcohol need to be replaced with the same number of ounces of water for proper hydration.

BUT no matter where you are in your fitness journey, LOVE your body. Cherish it. Thank it for where it is and where it's going to take you. STOP saying to yourself that you're ugly, or fat, or any of the other bullshit you tell yourself, and sure as fuck, don't let anyone else tell you those things. Like anything in life, look at the goal, create a plan, and be consistent with it. If you fall off the path, get back on, and thank the Universe that you have the strength to hit reset anytime you need. Whatever you do, stop beating yourself up. There is no room for that when you live an inspired, make your dreams come true, kind of life.

You have this perfect, amazing body that is a cosmic system all of its own. There is an abundance of oxygen, blood, and heart pumping goodness, and you don't even have to think about it. Your body just automatically does all of this on its own. All these functions are just given to you from a perfect Source who thinks only in terms of ideal health. Your body was meant to heal itself and your body was meant to MOVE. Whether it's ten minutes a day or an hour a day, make time to move that perfect body of yours that was created with love. Love your body, love yourself. Remember that you are perfect because you came from perfection.

I beg of you, go to the mirror and take a good long look, then smile. You're made of epic, cosmic shit. You are unique; you offer special gifts and talents to this planet that other people can't. You're made of stardust, so own that shit.

When you love yourself, you are free.

Suggestions:

1. We have a tendency to be so hard on ourselves because of outside expectations. Today, and from now on, look in that mirror of yours and remind yourself that you are indeed a beautiful piece of creation

intended to be on this planet right here, right now, for a perfect reason.

2. Begin to consciously change the conversations you have with yourself. This may seem small, but what you focus on expands. The Law of Attraction feeds off of feeling. It's essential to begin to train yourself to feel more of the emotions you genuinely want in your life. If you start to have negative self-talk, recognize that your ego isn't real, and shift the conversation to serve you and your higher purpose.

3. This journey you're on is really all about you. It's about others too, yes, but in a different way than you may currently believe. Bottom line, you aren't responsible for how others perceive you or react to you. You cannot control others. The only thing you can control is yourself.

2. Forgiving Yourself Is A Magic Pill of Awesome

Speaking of being free, let's go back and talk about the past for a little bit. It's extremely necessary for us to dig out of our own bed of shit to make us unfuckwithable and live up to our true potential. We all have messy pasts unless you don't (I'd love to know your secret). We've all heard the saying before: "You are not the mistakes you've made." It's true. Look, we've ALL done things we are far from proud of, but honestly, those are all things that have made us the people we are today. I mean, I have a fucking laundry list of skeletons in this closet of mine, but thankfully, we have that kick-ass option to let it fucking go once and for all.

It is not okay, nor was it ever intended, for us to relive, day after day, the mistakes we've made in our life or the mistakes others have made which we've carried around with us. Holding onto these things causes significant damage to our bodies due to the stress it creates, emotionally, spiritually, and physically. Mistakes, in reality, are simply lessons learned on the road to enlightenment and badassery. If you do something shitty, learn from it, thank the Universe for it, and then be an example of the freedom that comes from forgiving yourself and others. Don't beat yourself up over and over again. You need these things in life to grow into the amazingness that you are. Now, if you keep making the same mistakes over and over again, you probably need to have a real conversation with yourself on what it is you're struggling with and why you continue to do something that doesn't make you feel good about yourself. However, I believe we will keep getting lessons until we learn them. Not for the sake of others, but for the evolution of our own self.

For the sake of letting bygones be bygones, let's say you go through this process of forgiving yourself, no matter what, for the sake of humanity; DO NOT let anyone take that away from you. I've had ridiculous arguments with exes or friends of the past, and as they've not been on the same spiritual level as me, they've attempted to make me continuously feel wrong about something or have tried to make me relive past mistakes. Hell, over half the fucking time, my past mistakes had absolutely nothing to do with them AT ALL. Please, I beg of you, walk away from those people as fast as you can.

Think about it for a moment. Do you have those kinds of people in your life? Are you letting other people dictate your 'letting the past go' feelings? Don't. DO NOT let anyone bully you or convince you that you are a bad person based on something you've done in the past. I did this for years and years. But as I've gotten a little older, grown a little bit wiser, I now refuse to let the insecurities or ignorant attitudes of other people dictate who the fuck I am or what my intentions are. And I have to hold myself accountable to those same standards. Yesterday was yesterday. I, too, should not and will not bring up past mistakes of others to make myself feel "better" than them. I am just as guilty, but I know now, so I can consciously make different decisions.

In the nitty-gritty of honesty, I once had a brief affair with a married man. True story. Shitty as it sounds. I let a good friendship, something I cared about, get a little out of hand. I had just gone through a divorce, and there were issues in his marriage, and we both made a mistake. We had a mature conversation about letting it go, and we moved forward. The kicker is, it came out years later. His wife who, over the years, had come to be a good friend of mine, and who I genuinely cared and still care for, found out. Other people knew because of the small circle we lived in. Hearts were deeply broken. I'm still being judged for that mistake by some people. However, the beauty is that I've been forgiven by all parties involved, and their marriage is stronger than ever. Most importantly, I've forgiven myself.

I share this with you because I don't care about your judgment. There are a lot of people who have dealt with infidelity. I know the power I hold inside of this spiritual life of mine. I know the lessons I needed to learn from that experience. I also know the lessons the couple had to deal with through all of it as well. Most importantly, I know my truth. I've done a million shitty things, but I'm not that person anymore. TODAY and every day, I forgive myself for my past. I get to wake up each day to a brand-new beginning. My hope and intention for you is to learn to do the same and live in this freedom as well. You are not your past. And anyone who wants to hold that against you can fuck right off. You do not need them in your life.

Dale Carnegie said it best, "Any fool can criticize, condemn, and complain—and most fools do. But it takes character and self-control to be understanding and forgiving."

Suggestions:

1. Take some time today and think about something you've been angry about or have been beating yourself up over. Get in a quiet space and bring it into your awareness. Feel how it feels in your body, and then embrace it. After you've shown it love and attention, thank it for the lesson it had to teach, and then let it go.

2. Stop looking backward. You can't change the things you've done in the past. What you can do is in THIS moment begin to align with powerful, positive energy that lifts you to a higher place or a higher consciousness. This gives YOU the power, which you ALREADY HAVE, to dictate how you behave in the future.

3. Stop judging yourself because, I promise you, your Creator is not judging you one bit. We will talk about this later in the book, but you must know for now that where you and I and every piece of creation in this entire Universe came from is a loving, peaceful, and free-spirited, Source. It knows nothing of lack, fear, good, bad, or judgement. It only knows love. So, forgive yourself, because it's all you. The only thing that matters at the end of the day is the love you have for yourself and spreading love and peace to all of humanity around you.

3. Forgiving Others Makes Even More Magic

So, while we are forgiving ourselves, we also have to forgive whatever and whoever else that we're holding onto. Yes, I know this can be a hard one. I get it. When Jesus said, "Forgive them, Father, for they know not what they do," in Luke 23:32, there will always be absolute truth to those words. Now, I'm not a religious person. Facts are, Jesus walked the Earth, we have a historical record of him, and he was a teacher and enlightened leader at the time. However, people couldn't handle it, which is why he was tortured...all in the name of religion and the need for control. Jesus spoke up, knowing that he came from his Father, Source, God, and the Universe. He used words of wisdom beyond what the ego-driven, power-hungry leaders of the time could possibly comprehend. That truth couldn't be handled by a lot of people. For many, this is still the case.

However, back to forgiving other people...it's essential to understand that most people live in a state of unconsciousness. They're so caught up in their own ego and emotions that they genuinely don't know what the fuck they're doing. They go about life caught up in any kind of drama you can imagine, continually battling themselves and other people, and only focusing on the injustices in this world. Whether someone is personally suffering or suffering within a group, the drama of the ego is real. In order to rise above all that bullshit, you have to be in tune with yourself. You have to honestly know how your actions and attitudes effect those around you.

Some of the best advice I've ever received was from my friend and numerologist Joni. Joni was introduced to me by my friend, Hazel Walker, at a very crucial stage in my life. Joni told me this: "It's NONE of your business what other people think about you." (You'll be getting one-liners from her throughout this book. She's a WISE, WISE woman).

In all seriousness, live by this. While you're learning to live in a world of love, forgiveness, kindness, and all the things we absolutely need to be in tune with in the Universe, we also have not one, but TWO middle fingers to give to anyone who needs them, and plenty of people need them. It's OKAY to walk away from the people who do not encourage you to be a better you. Fuck anyone and everyone who has anything to say about you. It's NONE of your business what they think. In those heavy moments that WILL absolutely happen until you start attracting better things and people into your life, you have to remember to let go and step away from your bruised ego. Always remember that small minds talk about people, average minds talk about events, but GREAT minds talk about ideas. Please be a great mind. You'll be doing EVERYONE and the Universe a considerable favor. That's when shit can really change.

Always remember that other people's judgment of you is not a reflection of YOU, but truly a reflection of them. Dr. Wayne W. Dyer, one of my biggest spiritual influencers, used to say, "What other people do is their karma. How you react is yours." Silently thank them for reminding you that you're strong and you know who you are. Thank them and the Universe for the lessons you're learning. If you've fucked up or fucked them over, ask them for forgiveness, make amends, and then let that shit go. People are in your life for a reason, a season, or a lifetime… It may be cliché, but it's definitely true. This state of mind and consciousness paves the way to making yourself unfuckwithable.

It takes a big person to forgive someone once they've hurt you. Sometimes we feel like holding onto a grudge is good, whether we've cut those people out of our lives or not. However, when we hold onto those bitter feelings and constantly think about that person and their wrongdoings, we're the ones who suffer in the long run. You've heard this. You know this. Choosing to forgive someone is about you, not about them. When you forgive others, you're letting the Universe know that you're ready to move on and take your own path. Then, the Universe can see that, and make epic shit happen, because your forgiveness is operating at a way higher frequency than your ego drama.

One of the biggest challenges in my life was to forgive my ex-boyfriend's Mom. I loved this woman, and would have done anything for her, but for some reason, she just really enjoyed being a miserable person to me. One time, while on vacation, she told me I needed to recognize my place in the food chain, and it was at the bottom. Then she called me a whore for telling her son what she said. She said so many hurtful things to me over the years and would go out of her way to be harmful, but I always forgave her. While it all still hurts a little, being able to forgive her and her shit was one of the most freeing and liberating things I have ever done. She is dealing with her own life issues, and I've finally let it all go. I still think about her, but I no longer get angry when her name is mentioned. Now, I meditate on good wishes for her and wrap her up with love in my mind. I always will because forgiving her has set me free. Forgiving everyone who has said or done mean things to hurt me has set me free and it will do the same for you.

The bottom line is this: Stop being a victim of the past. We've all been hurt. We've all been devastated to the point of tears. We've all had our hearts taken, stomped on, spit-up, and shat out. We all have allowed our own behavior along with the behavior of others to damper our days, weeks, and sometimes years. Some of you may spend exuberant amounts of time imagining those conversations about that perfect "going off" moment we would all like to have with said people. I know I have. And damn, do I get them good in my mind. Man, fuck that. It's time to take control of your thoughts and take control of your mind.

There is NOTHING positive that can come out of negative thoughts. That's why it's imperative to your well-being and sound mind to forgive and let the past go. If you continue to play the victim, rather than take responsibility for your past, you will only keep the cycle of negativity going. It's a universal fact. What you focus on expands, and what you think about, you attract. The definition of insanity is doing the same thing over and over again and expecting different outcomes. The same is true when we think the same thoughts and expect a different life.

To stop being a victim and blaming other people's behavior for the predicament that you're currently in, you must take some damn responsibility for the fact that you ALLOWED these things to happen. Granted, some people have endured severe emotional and physical trauma that could take years of therapy to recover from. Examples include rape, physical abuse, sex trafficking, etc. I would never begin to diminish the pain that anyone has endured, and I pray that if you are someone who has been a victim of needless violence, that you are seeking help to overcome it. However, I urge you to eventually find forgiveness for those who have hurt you. This will set you free.

For those who just hold onto little things, whether it's someone talking bad about us, or spreading lies or rumors, people who have cheated on us or cheated us out of something we thought we needed, here's an excellent spot to remind you, you can't lose something that is good for you.

If you remember every day that you can't lose anything that's good for you, it allows for a glimmer of hope that your thoughts can change, and therefore your reality can change. After all, the hope of this book is to make you unfuckwithable. That way, you don't give a shit, in the sweetest, most powerful sense of that term. Don't let the behavior of other people affect you.

I've experienced asshole people my entire life, which I look at now as the biggest blessing. As a young girl, going to a private Baptist school, I had pretty much the same twenty-five or so kids with me from preschool through the 7th grade. I wanted to be a cheerleader more than anything from the 4th - 6th grades. My older sisters (we're all four years apart) were cheerleaders at the school, and I wanted to carry on that tradition. Plus, I was good at it.

At this particular school, you could "try out" for cheerleading, but your ability had little to do with making the squad. They based a lot of "making it" on something called "attitude." I made the cheerleading squad in the 4th grade, which, for some reason, was on a 'probationary' term. I didn't get it. While I was one of the best cheerleaders because of my mad skills, I apparently had a "bad attitude." This made no sense to me because I was a great student. I was involved in school, I did my best to play nice, but I never made the squad again. Thank you, Universe, because I'd much rather be a rocker than a cheerleader anyway. However, I never understood why a few of the parents of my friends just didn't like me. I was often excluded. My Mother, to this day, apologizes to me for not taking me out of that school sooner than she did.

What I know now, as I have a teenage daughter who is talented and brilliant and kind, is that some parents just love drama. It's weird to think of myself as the same age as those parents were back then. I can't even imagine what went through their heads daily. In that lesson, I vowed to be on the up and up, especially when it comes to other people's kids. Be love. Be the change. That's what I do.

Something else I experienced; I was molested by a great uncle in my family when I was fourteen. Something as innocent as a "motorcycle ride" turned into being one of the most awkward experiences of my life. I still remember it so vividly in my head. And the shame I felt after. I finally shared with my family what had happened about a year later, but it took some serious letting go to get over it. The biggest lesson I learned is that I can't hold onto any of that anymore. And you can't hold on to any of your shitty baggage either.

Life isn't always fair or kind, but you do have control over how you accept and play the hand you've been dealt. You certainly have the power to move on from the past and manifest an abundant, prosperous future, if that's what you so desire. The first step comes by thinking differently and forgiving the past. Let. That. Shit. Go. And forgive because forgiveness is like a fucking unicorn.

Life Changes When You Lose The Chip On Your Shoulder

Have you ever met someone who is always angry or has a "the world is out to get me" attitude? You know those people on your Facebook newsfeed that are incessantly pessimistic? You see how they are always attracting negative energy into their lives and putting it out there for the world to see? Are YOU one of those people? If so, please stop. You're only going to keep attracting the crap.

In my 20s, I worked in different tattoo shops around the country as a body modification artist, aka body piercer. One of the reasons I got out of the industry is because so many artists were so angry all the time or thought they were better than everyone else. The chips on people's shoulders are fucking ugly. Lose them. It's really that simple. It's a choice.

If you feel you are getting hurt time and time again, or if you feel like everyone lets you down, it's time to start examining your role and responsibility in this along with what you can do to create change.

I recently went through a situation where I always felt hurt, intimidated, let down, and disrespected; this was my relationship with my ex. I finally had to make a change. I was literally living the insanity of doing the same things and expecting different results. The morning I made the difficult decision to leave my ex, the sayings "You can't lose something that is good for you," and "you can't keep living in insanity," kept repeating over and over in my head. Reminding myself over and over finally gave me the courage to make a change.

I was in a toxic relationship. The person I was with always had a chip on his shoulder. He complained, he placed blame, he was jealous and insecure, and he projected his feelings of inferiority onto others, especially me. At the same time, he also did everything he could to help support me financially while I was pursuing my music career. I felt like I had an obligation to never leave, despite my unhappiness and the inner nagging feeling that something wasn't right. I felt like I needed to help get him out of his current state of mind and teach him a different way of life. I always encouraged this, which continuously backfired on me as he accused me of acting like I was "better than everyone else." However, I knew better. I knew my heart. I knew my intention. I couldn't live like that any longer.

I remember, at one point in time, I loved this man. I was IN love with him, but time, alcohol, and substance abuse, along with living in an unhealthy environment, eventually took its toll. It was time for me to go. So I did. It was one of the hardest things ever, especially as he begged and cried and tried to convince me things would change. The thing was, I had heard this a million times before. I always stayed, and things would be okay for a while, then go back to the usual. That was my insanity. So, I had to leave.

I really need to express again that this was not easy to do. It took everything for me to take a stand for myself and make a change. The chip on my ex-boyfriend's shoulder, like the ones I had seen in many of the environments I had allowed myself to be in in the past, made it easier for me to walk away. Chips make people ugly over time, and after a while, they really affect you.

Finding Yourself

The reason I am so passionate about pushing the message to "find yourself" is because, not only does this make you unfuckwithable, it makes you a better person for everyone who is currently in your life. That's not even including the people you're going to attract into your life out of pure Universal law.

When you finally soften and lose the chip you've had for so long, you begin to see other people and things differently. When you start to give love and respect, love and respect start flowing your way. And if the people you currently surround yourself with continue to be Debbie Downers in your life, it's time to cut them loose. I've left jobs, friendships, romantic relationships, and cities to find peace and light in my life. I am no longer stuck in any situation. Also, the right people are coming to me because I continually thank God for the abundant friendships that are in store for me. That's the place I live in now.

While I went through the breakup, my ex learned some serious lessons. He's now doing really well, and his change in attitude toward himself, others, and the Universe has spawned some vast and compelling opportunities in his life. I hope he continues on that path.

So, Linds, how do we do this? How can I just let the chip go? The best way to lose the chip on your shoulder is to first recognize that there is one. What makes you tick? What upsets you? What are you REALLY afraid of? We do many insane things out of fear but don't even realize fear is at the wheel. Do the things you hold onto really fucking matter, or do you let your ego drive you? Will it matter in six months? Will it matter in six years? Probably not. This all goes back to getting really fucking real about who you are and what you want in this lifetime, and forgiving yourself and others.

You deserve a passionate life that you love. Chips won't ever give you that because they are in direct conflict with everything the Spirit and Universe stand for. You get what you ask for, and what you focus on expands.

YOU are no BETTER than ANYONE. We are all human beings with beautiful Spirits. Let's always remember that.

Suggestions:

1. Throughout the day, the moment you get down on yourself – pause, take a breath, and remember that you are okay, and everything is going to BE okay.

2. Remember that no one is perfect, even those you admire or put on a pedestal have issues they're working through.

3. When you want to relive a past moment or experience that is painful, coming from your actions or those of others, take a second and remind yourself that you can't change or control what other people do or have done, or what is happening in the world around you. What you CAN control is your reaction. By forgiving yourself and others, you're opening up new space in this abundant Universe for something even better than you can possibly imagine.

4. *When the Going Gets Tough*

I know that loving yourself, forgiving yourself, and forgiving others can be a daunting task. It was for me, so I'd like to take a step back and share with you some things I incorporated into my life to help me overcome some of the issues I had with all of these things.

When I started acknowledging that there was a presence bigger than myself that was on my side, my life shifted, and the way I looked at things began to change. I began to pray. I began to meditate. I started reading books about spirituality, and I started writing down things I was grateful for. I needed a complete overhaul in the way I was viewing things because my past was so jaded with religious bullshit that I took rebellion to the complete opposite end of the spectrum. It wasn't until I opened my mind up to the differences between religious dogma, and true oneness and spirituality, that things began to change for me.

I began to pray. Not on my knees kind of pray, but real talk with God, the Universe, or whatever you want to call it. I know, I know. This may be a tall order for you, especially if you call yourself agnostic or atheist. I get it. I really do. When someone would tell me they were "praying for me," I honestly would get all pissy in my head and think, "Why don't you do something that matters, like actually

HELP?" I totally related to comedian Hannibal Buress's bit on this subject. It goes like this:

> Yeah, I don't like it when people say they'll pray for me. 'I'll pray for you.' Are you gonna pray for me? So basically, you're going to sit around at home and do nothing while I struggle with a situation, so don't pray for me. Make me a sandwich or something cuz I'm very upset right now, I can't make my own sandwich right now so that would be cool if you made me a sandwich instead of praying. That's very lazy. 'Well, we'll keep you in our thoughts.' With all the other bullshit in your head, no. Keep me outta your thoughts cuz I hear some of the stuff you talk about, and if that's close to the stuff you're thinking about, I don't wanna be around that at all so keep my family and me out of your thoughts unless you're thinking about making us sandwiches.

Me typing out the words doesn't do it justice AT ALL, but it's so funny. Please check it out when you get a chance.

Hopefully, you get the point. That was my attitude about prayer and my attitude toward other people who would say they were praying. My past, personal thought on prayer was that it was a religious thing that may work or may not work. Honestly, I was so anti-religion and rebellious that I didn't consider much other than having a dumb chip on my shoulder regarding anyone who prayed. Really, what was all my fuss about? After all, we could all benefit from a few extra people giving God a few kind words on our behalf.

It's funny because, on my spiritual journey, it's easy for old thought patterns to creep in at the most awkward times, but I have to immediately reverse those thoughts. While you won't typically hear me say, "I'm praying for you," deep down inside I will be. I call that good vibes, and I hope to help you in any way I can. Plus, I don't really think prayer is about you (other people). It's about me. It's about MY speaking and time with the Universe to bring about a higher frequency that I'm sharing with you from afar. I know that may sound confusing or not make sense, but my hope is that one day it will.

Here's what I've learned since I decided to get real about change and actually educate myself, not on religion, but on spirituality. I no longer believe prayer is a process of asking your Higher Power for the fulfillment of what you are lacking, which is how I was raised. A typical prayer in my home was "Lord, please help us to _____," get the job, get the extra money, work something out, or whatever you wish, you insert in the blank. Basically, something was lacking, so we were to ask God for the fulfillment of the lacking thing.

I now see prayer as a time to give thanks for what we are about to receive and for what we currently have in abundance. It's about acknowledging that we have faith that everything is as it should be, and will continue to be so, as long as we are in alignment with, or working towards alignment with, our highest selves. It's about giving thanks for your vision that you're about to create for yourself as you read these pages. I have come to believe and know that there's a VERY specific way to pray to create change. We can only be in line with our highest Energy when we focus on the language of our Creator, who knows nothing of lack. It's really about changing the dialogue. (As far as the "name" you use for prayer, I personally believe it doesn't matter because our Creator is the ENERGY and the SOURCE who created us, so name or no name, when you align with the Energy of the Universe, your Spirit is heard).

In *The Power of Intention* by Dr. Wayne Dyer, there are so many examples of how to think about things and change your inner dialogue, so it's in full alignment with Spirit. As a matter of fact, I highly recommend taking the time to read that book. It changed me in so many ways that I give it to so many people in my life. Dr. Wayne Dyer gets to points that I won't touch in this book, but I promise, if you read any of his work, you'll be crazy inspired. Reading books of this nature helps you have constant receptivity to the message of Spirit.

Now, as I said, some of you reading this may want nothing to do with God. I used to be in your shoes. Again, this is not about religion. This is not about Jesus. This is not about Buddha. This is about connecting to the Energy that CREATED you. Because trust me, you're the one who chose to be here at this moment in time, going through the things you're going through (good or bad), to learn the lessons you're supposed to learn on this go around. Through prayer, we're able to have an open dialogue with our Source.

Whether you believe it or not, we were ALL born in Spirit. That Spirit is more in tune with us when we come to it in gratitude, peace, and love. It's the Law of Attraction. The Universe is continuously listening to us, giving us exactly what we're focused on, giving us exactly what we ask for. Change your thoughts for the better, change your dialogue for the better, then your life begins to change, you guessed it, for the better.

Another major factor in my change was meditation, which is very different from prayer. I believe prayer is a time of expressing thanks and speaking to the Universe about real shit in your life, and meditation is when you shut the hell up. I believe this is perhaps one of THE most important things that will help change your life. I can't express enough the importance of this practice and the change you will see in your life once you open up to quietness and stillness. I am not a meditation expert. Quite frankly, I've only begun regularly practicing in the past few years. I'm in awe of how this practice has spawned considerable changes in my life, including the creation of this book.

My daily processes of prayer, meditation, and writing are things I absolutely must do to feel complete now. There is nothing on this planet that can compare to the ideas that have through these processes, along with the love, joy, and peace that fill my heart and soul.

Meditation has allowed me to be in control of my emotions, no matter what is going on in my environment. It's not about "ohms," it's not about getting weird. It's not even about the amount of time, per se. What it IS, is a chance to quiet your mind and get you in touch with your soul, your true presence, which will then allow you to get in touch with your true passion and purpose for your journey, which is here now.

A free, downloadable app that I've grown very fond of is called Insight Timer. It's my jam when it comes to meditation. Sometimes I use the guided meditation, sometimes I do my own Japa meditation with music from Spotify. Sometimes I use meditation to put all my dreams out into the quantum field. I can't express the importance of meditation in your personal journey to badassery and unfuckwithableness. Meditation, quiet time with the Energy of the Universe, helps us co-create who we are today, and is a place where

TRUE magic happens.

I've known many people who skip this step, but I wouldn't recommend it. Yes, things can happen that are great. Still, I'm telling you from personal experience that crazy, unimaginable shit happens when you get personal with the Energy that created you and surrounds you.

Dr. Wayne Dyer calls this "getting in the gap," and has an incredibly short book on Japa meditation. I highly recommend it. Another considerable assistance in my journey at the beginning of my meditation practice was the 21-day meditations by Oprah Winfrey and Deepak Chopra. These are offered free about four times a year. You can also purchase them online, and they're brilliant. With time, you'll come to cherish and crave this special time to envision, manifest, and believe in your cosmic force.

There is no right or wrong way to meditate. I have my go-to spot and position, but I don't do it at the same time every day. Sometimes I lay down, sometimes I do it outside or on a couch. Hell, I've even fallen asleep meditating. That's okay. The main thing is I DO it every day. You can do it sitting up, lying down, in an airport or in a quiet place of your choosing. You can do it for ten seconds, two minutes, five minutes, 20 minutes, or throughout your day. One of the points of meditation (breathing, focusing on our breath, on the Spirit of ourselves and the Universe, which is one) is taking the time to pay attention to your breath and bringing you back into the now, since our mind loves to wander and create the crazy, unconsciousness most people exist in.

So, you may be wondering why meditating is so crucial, besides what I just explained about tapping into the awesomeness of the Universe. There are both spiritual and physical benefits of meditating. In his book, *Getting in the Gap*, Dr. Wayne Dyer explains how meditation has been proven to help reduce stress, cultivates a sense of peace, eliminates fatigue, slows the aging process, improves memory, helps us to find clarity of purpose, and even helps us heal. Are you sold yet? Let me remind you, this shit is FREE. So why would you not even TRY it?

Furthermore, the spiritual benefits are just as significant. Here is an excerpt from *Getting in the Gap*:

The paramount reason for making meditation a part of our daily life is to join forces with our sacred energy and regain the power of our Source (God). Through meditation, we can tap into an abundance of creative energy that resides within us, and a more meaningful experience of life, which enriches us permanently. By meditating, we come to KNOW God rather than ABOUT God.

Speaking from personal experience, this book idea was born out of meditation. The particular meditation I was going through at the time was from *The Abundance Book* by John Randolph Price, which I was doing for fifteen minutes a day for forty days, while continually reading books to get in touch with MY Source and true calling. Even more significant is that I'm writing a book with "fuck" in the title. You think I give a shit? This came from my Source to reach YOU right now. I've even had people in my family let me know how I was leaving out a lot of demographics by naming my book this. Ugh, whatever. I got this. The Universe has this. They don't. See, I'm becoming unfuckwithable as I'm going through this journey too.

As soon as I finish my daily practice of prayer and meditation, I write down at least five things I'm grateful for at that moment. Sometimes it's being thankful for my family, or a good night's rest, or for having a perfect body that heals itself and keeps everything flowing. Sometimes it's the people that are in my life who have kept me passionate for that day or the previous day. No matter what it is that I'm grateful for, that gratitude always starts my day off right. Sometimes it moves into more of a journal entry. But regardless, taking the time to write and focus on what IS working in your life rather than what's NOT working sets a completely different tone for your entire day. You're writing down gratitude. You're writing down blessings. When you are thankful, and in peace with all of these things, you will receive more of the same because what you focus on expands. Again, this IS the Law of Attraction.

For me, this writing has also been a unique way to learn more about who I am and where my heart is. It has also helped me center in on my vision as I've done different writing exercises to hone in on it. I ask that as you go through this book, you take the time to at least write out five things you are grateful for each day, as soon as you wake, or as soon as you complete your meditation time. I talk a lot about gratitude in the chapter "Gratitude Fucking Owns." But until we get there, baby steps, as you are growing into a bigger and better person. Writing down five things is a great first step.

I know we're just getting started, but another thing I'm going to encourage you to do is to read one thing a day that empowers you and helps you feel connected.

I know "self-help" books sound so uncool, but this isn't about labels, as we're getting to the point where we're dropping judgments of things. We need to get RID of labels and reading some REALNESS every day can help you do that. Taking 20-40 minutes each day to read books by great teachers, mentors, and colleagues is imperative in this process as we go on. I will reference many of these authors and spiritual teachers throughout the day(s) that you read this book. I encourage you to read their works and hear their lessons as soon as you get a chance. If you feel like you don't have that kind of time, please delete Facebook off of your phone and then talk to me.

One of my favorite sayings is, "Reading can cause serious damage to your ignorance." Constant education is a must, whether it be for your vocation or on your way to Inspired Badassery, so please take the time to read and learn more about being Inspired and being a better person. Reading will CHANGE YOUR LIFE. It can help spawn ideas. It can help you become aware of things you may not have considered in the past. We are here to be the best we can be, and that's one of the reasons you're reading this book. I still read and re-read books that speak to me. And btw, this is technically a self-help book so, cheers to you for picking it up.

Reading opens many doors, and for those of you who do not like to read, there are audiobooks. We all learn differently, and it doesn't matter how you get the information into your head, as long as you do it regularly.

Suggestions:

1. When you wake up each day, take a few moments to say, "Thank you." These two little words are really all you need to say. Acknowledge the Universe. Thank it for the new day and for another opportunity to help create a better environment.

2. Download the Insight Timer App to your phone. Find a space where you can be alone and start with just one minute. Relax your body, take a deep breath in, and in your mind, repeat the phrase, "So hum." This translates to "I Am." See if you can build on the one-minute time once you feel you are ready.

3. At any point in the day, when you feel overwhelmed or irritated, take five deep breaths, and write down five things you're grateful for. This helps put things into perspective and helps you to refocus with more clarity.

4. Carry a book with you that will help you grow. Even if you can only get in a page or two or just one chapter at a time, take a few moments for yourself and your growth. I am always reading at least one book, sometimes more at one time. I schedule reading time. I encourage you to as well.

5. *Love as Hard as You Can*

I have this saying I live by, "Live Hard...Love Harder. "It's been my motto for years. I've always claimed that Love is my religion. I grew up in a bible-thumping, Christian home, and was taught that there is a right and a wrong and no in-between. There were a million rules, and nothing "secular" could be in our home. No MTV (you know, that channel that used to play music videos), no music that wasn't God music, and church three times a week, on top of going to a private, Christian school. Gays were sinners, music was of the devil, and everything that was not in line with the church was a sin. I didn't get that shit. EVER. I still don't.

I never, in my child's mind growing up in the '80s, thought there was anything wrong with the gay couple that lived across the alley from my childhood home. They were nice. They always said hi and waved to us, and at the time, my parents were not okay with them. I mean, my parents would wave and be nice, but then as soon as we walked into our home, there was the chitter-chatter of their "sin." I always felt like saying to my parents, "Yo, chill out, not your life, so who cares?"

I also never thought there was anything wrong with music that expressed feelings of love, hurt, or anger. It was all art to me. I never thought there was anything wrong with Debbie Gibson's

"Electric Youth" and her lyrics, "the future only belongs in the hands of itself, and the future is electric youth." However, my parents did. As a matter of fact, they took such offense to this teenage song that they took my cassette tape away from me, claiming it was "new age" thinking. And this didn't just stop with me. It affected my two older sisters as well. They took away Michael W. Smith from my oldest sister, and he was a Christian artist. It was insane! My family had major control issues, and we were barely able to listen to music. I remember sneaking around to listen to the radio with my sisters, and one of us would keep watch to see when they were pulling up the driveway so we could turn it off. And while my family thought they were doing their best, thankfully, I was able to escape the brainwashing and genuinely learn to love it all. Such is life. Fortunately, my family is no longer that crazy, only a little crazy, so it's a win all around. We've all evolved in some ways, even though we may not agree with each other's life choices. However, throughout my life with the experiences I've been able to have and process, and in the teachings I've come to believe in, I don't really believe in right or wrong because all right and wrong is based on ego. Sure, there are the fundamentals, but honestly, nothing is for me to judge anymore, and here's why.

In Dale Carnegie's book, *How to Win Friends and Influence*

People, he so eloquently describes judging in an 'off the cuff' kind of way. In the chapter "What Everybody Wants", he is explaining what he believes to be the magic phrase in eliminating an ill will, which is, "I don't blame you one iota for feeling as you do. If I were you, I would undoubtedly feel just as you do." He goes on to say:

> Take Al Capone, for example. Suppose you had inherited the same body and temperament and mind that Al Capone had. Suppose you had had his environment and experiences. You would then be precisely what he was – and where he was. For it is those things – and only those things – that made him what he was. The only reason, for example, that you are not a rattlesnake is that your mother and father weren't rattlesnakes.

And yes, this is an extreme example. I know there are examples of people growing up in the dimmest of conditions who did not make the same decisions as some of their peers. A beautiful thing about being human is having the free will to do whatever you choose to do. Should we judge other people when we haven't walked in their shoes? Or is it better to love instead? Do you enjoy it when people judge you?

I have experienced firsthand that when we live in Spirit and live in Love, there is only room for acceptance, peace, and inspiration. We learn that there is no better feeling or way to be once we experience that kind of acceptance, peace, and inspiration. This peace and contentment pour over to all other areas of our lives when we let go and let the Universe do its thing. It's fucking incredible.

It's insanely important to go about our day in a spirit of Love. That Love radiates at such a higher energy field than ANYTHING else. BE what you want to attract. Make it a priority to go about your day in Love, EVERY day. Be accepting of other people and how other people act. Be the person you want other people to be. Plant those Love seeds. Not to say you're not going to be challenged, because you will, but when you're conscious of what's happening, you truly can control your reactions to different scenarios so that your negative emotions don't consume you. Plus, you can be thankful for whatever lesson is there that you need to learn at that moment.

Love is the power to heal, to bond, to make things better. It not only impacts those around you, but it also impacts you and your health.

Suggestions:

1. Remember, when you are tempted to lash out or get offended, instead, offer Love and acceptance and see how it makes you feel.

2. For you to FEEL Love, you must BE Love.

3. Remember that you came from a place of pure Love and pure Intention. Once you tap into Love, you can change your life and the lives around you. Love is a choice.

6. *The Power of the Vision Board*

Have you ever heard of a vision board? Perhaps you have, perhaps you HAVE one. For those of you unfamiliar with it, it's basically a poster board with images and words that you put on it to create your "vision" for your life. I know it may sound completely silly, but I promise you, creating your own vision board is so worth it. Plus, it's fun to get creative with it.

When I began my spiritual journey back in 2009, my business and spiritual coach, Deseri Garcia, encouraged my coaching group to make vision boards for what we really wanted in our lives. I knew I wanted my dreams of becoming a successful, paid musician and songwriter to happen. I had also watched *The Secret* and *What The Bleep Do We Know?* and was reading about quantum physics and all of those things. I was around successful people who I felt were spiritually enlightened, and I wanted that successful attitude about life and abundance too. Also, I was having some seriously amazing things happen in my life, and I recognized the perfect orchestration of the Universe. It was actually starting to blow me away. I was watching true synchronicity happen in all areas of my life at that point, from the divorce I had just gone through, to the place I was able to move into, to a nonprofit I got to be a co-founder of, to the success of my band at the time, to the people I was meeting. I felt like an outside

Force was really working on my behalf.

A few months after the vision board suggestion, I decided to have a vision board making session at my place and invited my bandmates at the time to join me. Pretty much everything on that vision board was about my involvement in music. From stages to audiences to instruments, it was all on there. Besides that, I had some shoes I wanted, my dream home (the idea of how I wanted it to look), and how I envisioned interacting and being with the partner of my dreams. But the point is, it was fun. I put down my "wishes," my ideals, and how I wanted my life to be.

That was YEARS ago. Well, on October 14, 2014, the singer of one of my favorite bands in the entire world, a band called Cold, sent me a tweet asking me to call him, as he had sent his number to me via Facebook. (The wonders of social media…)

Now, I have to let you know that this band is so insanely special to me that I have a tattoo of the spider that is on their second album (which went Gold), *13 Ways to Bleed Onstage* from the year 2000. To top THAT off, when they released their third album, *Year of the Spider* (which also went Gold), they asked their fans to send in their spider tattoos. I had my oldest sister, Heather, take some photos (on a real camera, and actually placed these developed photos in an envelope because this was only 2001), and I sent them in. My photo made it into that album sleeve and is literally NEXT to the member whom I replaced as their bassist. I do not believe this is coincidence. In fact, Scooter, our singer, had no idea that photo was me placed in that album over a decade earlier when the album was released. This is true poetry and true vision. Talk about manifesting!

As I've been living in Temecula, California, and just finished recording my first album with this incredible band, I made a vision board for the band. It's in our writing room. If you're interested in the entirety of this grand story, I go into it at the end of this book.

I've been crazy fortunate enough to know what I've wanted to do since I was a little girl. I wanted to be in music. That is what I've strived for. I had a vision. And we can thank that Electric Youth album when I was a child because I literally wanted to do THAT.

Lewis Howes released a book in 2015 called *The School of Greatness*, which made him a New York Times Bestselling author. His book is all about finding your greatness, having a vision, and going beyond your own limitations. He says, "Beyond those limitations is where greatness lives. If you don't figure out what you want in life and who you want to be, you will most likely feel trapped within those limitations. No path to greatness has ever involved settling for less than what you really want."

What Lewis said should really make you think. Are you settling? Do you know what you REALLY want to do? What are you passionate about? In a perfect world that you co-create, what does that look like? What are you doing? Where are you living, how are you making money (doing what you love to do)? I will repeat this quote that spoke to me from *Living An Inspired Life* by Dr. Wayne Dyer, multiple times: "There is nothing more powerful than an idea whose time has come."

What I'm asking is, have you ever taken the time to think about YOUR vision that YOU want for yourself? It doesn't matter how realistic you think your dream or vision is.

If you have a passion for something or are inspired to DO something, there IS a way because our Source doesn't just give us those passions and desires for shits and giggles. I encourage you to really explore your dreams, and to create your reality based around them. I also encourage you to pick up Lewis's book because he has a fantastic story of his dream, how it wasn't working out EXACTLY the way he envisioned, and how he made some changes and is now living one hell of an incredible life. He was even on *The Ellen Show*. That's how badass he is.

Now, let's take your dream to a spiritual level. I certainly know my dream of playing in a rock band was a spiritual thing because it goes beyond ego for me. Just like me wanting to write successful books goes beyond ego. Dr. Wayne W. Dyer, in his book, *I Can See Clearly Now*, says,

From a distance, I can see the truth in the idea that when I follow my excitement, I align myself with who I am as an infinite being. The excitement or feeling of inner bliss that arises when I contemplate what I truly know I must do is God-realization. When I stay in that state of following my bliss, everything I undertake is not only going to be effortless but even more significantly, I will be fully supported by the Universe as well.

Do you see that? Do you know when you follow what you TRULY love to do, and when you are aligned with the Universe, it literally wants to hand those dreams and desires to you. Yes, it takes effort on your part. I mean, I had to learn to play musical instruments, and I had to take the initiative and time to write this book, but the Universe knows my true desires and will support my efforts. And because you are made of the same stuff I am, the same applies to everything in your life. You just have to believe in the magic.

I encourage you to stop what you're doing, go to the store, grab up some magazines, and anything you can think of... words, photos, dream kitchen, dream car, anything you can imagine, glue that shit down on a poster board, and let the magic happen. Look at it every day and be, act, and feel as if it is so. Live in that vision, but most importantly, FEEL what it will feel like while having grace and gratitude for where you are today.

I understand that it may seem crazy and impossible. But once you get out of your own head and put faith in the Universe, magic happens.

Suggestions:

1. Take some time to think about what your dreams and visions are. What EXCITES you? What is something you love to do that makes you lose track of time? What does your home life look like? Think about YOU. Not your kids, partner, family, friends. YOU. Not to say they aren't included, but this is YOUR dream.

2. Get some magazines, some glue, some scissors, and a poster board. Don't think about it. Don't think it's silly or dumb. Just do it. Create a vision board that you can look at every single day. Even if what you put on, there isn't anywhere close to where you are, it's okay. It's okay to dream big and to trust that everything we want and desire is on the way. Once we begin to believe it, we'll start to see it, so long as you're connected in a higher vibration to our Source.

3. When you look at it, and it's what you REALLY want, pretend you're already there. FEEL it like you're already there. Just trust me on this.

7. Do the Fucking Work

"My ambition is handicapped by laziness."
— *Charles Bukowski*

Sometimes, we need to break down our dreams and our visions. Even to the hour. It's always good to ask yourself, "Where do I want to be in one year, two years, five years, or twenty years?" I've found that answers come to me easily when I get into meditation mode or Spirit mode. I'm personally amazed by what has inspired me to achieve my life calling, and I can promise you, it will have the same effect on you.

Regardless of what your dreams or visions are, you can meditate and try to manifest away, but that doesn't mean it will just come to you. Sure, ideas will come to you, inspiration will come to you, and even solutions to so-called "problems" or obstacles will come to you. That's all amazing. But to get to where you want to be, you HAVE to put in the work. There WILL be sacrifices, but all of them will be worth it.

A motivational, kick-ass saying that I have as a screen saver on my phone is this; "Why? Because I am made of stardust, I do epic, cosmic shit...that's why." No matter what your goals are, when you break it down, a dream can and should be a plan. What does that mean?

Wanna be a badass musician? Play your instrument as much as you can. Wanna write songs, then write them, and improve them. Wanna write a book? Start typing an hour a day until you can write for more extended periods. Wanna travel the world? Get a fucking passport. Wanna get in shape? There are a million apps, programs, and free resources available to you, but just get out and take a walk around the block to start. Wanna change lives? Surround yourself with people who are doing epic shit. But you HAVE to get out, and you HAVE to do the work.

When you begin to hear your life-calling (and you could have many because I promise you, I have a BUNCH), you'll be amazed at how easily things start to come to you. When I moved to California to play bass full-time, I was blown away by what I was able to do and will continue to be able to do, because I am in-Spirit, INSPIRED, and everything comes so much more easily than before. Things people think are impossible or super hard, come naturally. Also, when you're in alignment with your Source and the Universe, things kind of "fall into your lap," or you happen to meet the right people. There is no coincidence. It is pure cosmic synchronicity.

Have you ever met someone who seems to get everything they want and to be truly happy and to be making a difference in other people's lives? It's because they have a vision, a true vision, and are inspired to get up every day and act as if it is so. They do the work to make it so. One way to think of this is "preparation meets opportunity." There is no such thing as "overnight success." Everyone you believe is "lucky" put in years and years of preparation and hard work before they broke. You may do this too. People may believe that you were lucky, but you will know that you did the "work" both physically and spiritually. There is no luck involved, only the Universe, and your decision to listen to your heart and believe that you can do anything you want.

I am not the greatest musician technically, but my heart and work ethic are all in. I taught myself how to play guitar by learning a couple of chords out of a Mel-Bay guitar book twenty-two years ago that had belonged to my dad when he was that age. That's when I started to write my first songs. I'm now forty-one. All the bands I've been in, all the songs I've written, and all the albums I've had the opportunity to create or participate in have brought me to this point. It was not by luck or by chance that I am where I am today. It is because of the work I put into it. I know that I am the best I can be today, and tomorrow will be even greater as long as I do the work. I must practice. I must type words on a page to release this book. I have to take the time and do it.

It's a Friday night, and I'm sitting at home writing. I will sacrifice going out, seeing friends, being social, so I can get this to you for you to be inspired as well. No one is going to come to help me do this. No one is going to GIVE me a book deal. I will edit, re-edit, re-edit, and submit to so many agents that I need a list to track them all. I will and have gotten rejections from people, but I don't perceive rejection as failure. I see it as, "this is not the right person." Then I go right back to the drawing board and make whatever it is I'm doing even better.

Something I think about when I'm working on a goal is that all things in life take consistency. I encourage you to make a list every day. I don't know about you, but I love a good list. I especially love seeing one that's 80% checked-off by the end of the day. For me, a list keeps me in check. It keeps me on track, and it also makes me feel like I had a productive day.

There are also some pretty cool goal calendars out there. Commit 30 has one. One day, one week, or one month at a time, I encourage you to make lists. Having some accountability is imperative. A solid list is a good way to start. Plus, it's always good to organize, especially if you have a chaotic schedule and a family to run.

By the way, as you start evaluating the lists you have, keep this in mind. If you hate some of the things that are there, make a goal date of deleting those "to-dos." Anything that's on there that you have zero inspiration to do it, say no and stop doing it. It's that simple. The saying "if there's a will, there's a way" couldn't be more accurate in this case.

Today, commit to dedicate time to reaching your goals. Take time for YOURSELF. Meditate, get physical movement, and get in Spirit to make shit happen. No one else can do it for you.

Suggestions:

1. Recognize what's important to you. Make some short-term and long-term goals, then write them the fuck down. It doesn't matter how lofty, or how big, or how small the goal is, just get it on paper.

2. Once you write down your goals, write down a deadline for getting there. For example, I've hired an author coach to keep me accountable. We have a game plan. I know that I have three more months to do my edit of this book, build my platform, and have my proposal and query in tip-top shape. My deadline is three months.

3. Once you write down your deadline, write down how you're going to reach it. Going with my deadline example above, I am writing and editing for at least two hours a day. I time block these writing times. I only write for an hour at a time unless I'm on a roll. In between my writing time blocks, I have 30-minute time blocks to

rehearse the songs I'm going to be doing on tour and to do finger exercises on my bass. If I alternate between those two things, I accomplish things that are helping me reach my goal and keep me on track to meet the goal. Regardless of your goal, figure it out, write it down, then make a plan.

8. Give – Even When You Don't Know How You Can

I want to remind you again that you are a creation that came from a place of pure abundance. Please take this seriously, what you focus on EXPANDS. When you focus on needing more money or not having enough, you will always need more money, and you will never have enough. When you focus on what you don't have rather than what you DO have, you are not in alignment with the great, badass Force that wants you to have whatever it is you want or desire, and knows nothing of this ego-driven word called "lack."

Our Creator never intended for us to go without or to live a life of suffering. When we take things into our own hands, things have a funny way of going fucking awry. But when we're in alignment with this perfect, harmonious, energy force and live from a place of love, which means loving ourselves along our journey, magic shit happens.

With that said, one of the things we need to do as humans is GIVE. When we give from our hearts, we are then circulating love into the world. Love makes the world a better place. Giving without expecting anything in return can truly make your heart feel full, and rest assured, it will come back around because that's the vibe of the Universe. That's the Law of Attraction, and you can't fuck with how it all works.

I have a bulletin board that I look at every day with notes to myself on it. These are similar to the ones I've already asked you to make. One of the cards on my board is, "Give every morning." For me, it always starts with giving thanks. Once I start, then I figure out what else I can do. I never know what it's going to be or if it's going to be monetary or a text or a phone call, but I listen to my heart. What I can tell you is this practice is improving the hell out of my life, and I listen to Spirit to tell me what to do.

Giving comes in so many forms. It doesn't have to be monetary. Give your time, give your prayers and blessings, give some flowers, give some kindness and love. Give a smile. Hold a door open for someone. Send an encouraging text or make a phone call. Let someone know that they're special and that you are thinking of them. Be IN the moment.

I recently read a great article from one of Inc.com's contributing editors, Jeff Haden, entitled "Here's What Happened When I Complimented Everyone I Met for an Entire Day." It was an incredible read about Haden stepping outside of his comfort zone to make a change in people's lives that day. I'm sharing it with you with Jeff's permission. It moved me, so I hope it moves you as well. *No one gets enough praise. No one gets enough recognition. The reason is simple: Very few of us praise and recognize people as often as we should. I know I don't.*

So in the spirit of challenging myself (like when I was foolish enough to do 5,000 pushups in one day), I decided I would compliment everyone I ran into for an entire day--even just in passing, whether I knew them or not, whether it seemed socially appropriate or not...and whether or not I could think of something (anything) I could compliment them about.

While that might sound easier than doing 5,000 pushups, for me, it wasn't. I'm fairly shy and don't go out of my way to speak to people I don't know. (You might even argue that I go out of my way not to speak to people I don't know).

And here's how that little experiment went.

The Rules

Challenges work best when you impose structure, helping you stay on track and reducing the temptation to lose resolve and rationalize that you should change your goal midstream.

For this challenge, the structure was simple:

- *If I made eye contact with someone, I had to compliment them in some way...*

- *... and to make sure I never chickened out, I had to actively try to make eye contact. I couldn't intentionally look away.*
- *But I didn't have to compliment people already having a conversation, or on the phone, or wearing headphones.*
- *And I couldn't hide away all day. I had to go out into the world at least four times.*

So with that in mind...

Morning

The first few were really easy.

I was rolling the trash out to the street and saw my neighbor. She has a great collection of plants and flowers, so I said, "I'm always impressed by how beautiful your plants are. You have a real gift." Her face lit up. I don't think I made her day, but I do think I helped get her day off to a good start.

Then I went for a quick walk on the beach. Since it's fall, many of the people I met were walking their dogs or throwing balls into the surf for them to retrieve. "You have a beautiful dog," I said to the first one. He smiled and I realized I had complimented his dog, not him. Although many dog owners don't see a difference...still.

So I followed up with, "She always seems so happy. You must take really good care of her." He beamed and I realized I was right: Complimenting a person's dog (or child or car or whatever) is nice, but making the compliment personal makes a bigger impact.

So that's what I did. I told one man he had done an amazing job training his dog. I complimented a lady on what a great job she did grooming her dog. I felt pretty smug. Complimenting people was easier than I thought.

Then, off in the distance, I saw a fit, pretty, 20-something young woman headed my way. No dog. No third person-ish thing to compliment. Uh-oh.

I didn't want to be that guy, that older guy who goes around randomly complimenting young women and comes off creepy and, well, icky. I started to walk slower. I was thinking furiously but had nothing.

Then, from about 20 feet away, she made eye contact and smiled; not a half smile, not an automatic "good morning" smile, but a big, genuine smile.

I smiled back and said, "Thanks."

"For what?" she said.

"Lots of times when I'm walking people don't even make eye contact. I've always thought that was kind of rude. You seem so happy and saying hi was really nice."

She smiled even bigger and said, "How could I not be happy when I'm out here? Have a great day."

I know: What I came up with was pretty lame. But I like to think she walked away feeling good about herself, if only for a moment or two, which was the whole point of the exercise.

And I felt pretty good about myself, too, at least until I later led with, "Your daughter is really cute," only to be told, "Thank you, but he's a boy." Oh well.

Afternoon
Except for a few miscues, by this point I was rolling. I had learned to quickly size people up and pick out something obvious to

compliment how they cared for their animals, how they landscaped their yards, even how they dressed.

Yep: I even managed to whip out a, "That is such a pretty sweater-- I wish I had your fashion sense." (And to my surprise, she took it well.)

Then I went to the grocery store.

And let's just say that no one in a grocery store expects you to walk by and compliment them--not even the people who work there. And let's just say that, "Wow, you picked the perfect melon," isn't the right way to go. And neither is, "You look like you're on a mission. You seem extremely well organized."

And, "I wish I was as good at choosing the right steaks as you are," falls pretty flat.

And I wanted to give up. In some settings, it seemed, compliments are not just unexpected but also unwanted.

But I decided to try one more time, but with a twist. I decided to ask for help, because asking for help is implicitly complimentary: If I ask you for help, that means you know something I don't know, can do something I can't do...asking you for help is like saying, "I respect your knowledge/skill/experience."

That's what I did. I was in the seafood section and made eye contact with a 30-something woman. She didn't smile or nod (gulp!) but I forged ahead.

"I'm terrible at picking the right piece of salmon," I said. "Can I bother you for a second and ask you to help me?" And she did. She actually seemed to enjoy it.

And I got to say, "I really appreciate it. Thanks for helping me, and for being so nice."

So while I did have a couple tough moments, especially when I was standing in the checkout line behind an extremely frazzled father with three borderline out of control kids--the last thing he seemed to want was a random compliment--I made it out of the grocery store and through the parking lot with my compliment streak intact.
But I do have to admit I was relieved to get back in the car.

Evening
Dumb move No. 2: I went to the gym.

On one hand, it was easier: Most people wear headphones when they work out, so that eliminated them from my challenge.

On the other hand, moving from bench to squat rack to machines to free weights meant at some point I ran into almost everyone who was at the gym. Still. One guy was benching 325 pounds for reps. Easy compliment. A woman was doing a split and then laying all the way forward on the mat. Another easy compliment.

A guy jumped in and helped an apparent newcomer with his form on squats; presumptuous, yes, but also kind, since the way the guy was bending his back was a recipe for injury. When I ran into the Good Samaritan a few minutes later it was easy for me to say, "That was really nice of you to help him out." Then I found myself doing pull-downs near a guy doing seated rows. And I had nothing. Then I noticed the tattoo on his forearm. And I was in. "I really like your tattoo," I said.

He smiled, said thanks, and then spent the next five minutes talking all about it: where he got it, how he came up with the design, what it means to him…. And I realized that sometimes the easiest thing to compliment is the thing that people seem to want you to notice or are obviously proud of: a tattoo, a piercing, an unusual hair color…a

Porsche, a Hayabusa, a tricked-out truck...almost everyone has something they do or say or wear that they feel represents who they are inside.

All you have to do is look for it.

What I Learned

I can't say it was easy. Complimenting every person I ran into got easier, but never easy. It's not hard to compliment people you meet who are doing their jobs: grocery clerks, managers, front-desk people at the gym...saying thanks and telling them they did something well is fairly easy.

All you have to do is remember to do it.

Complimenting "random" people is harder but surprisingly rewarding. It was fun to watch people's faces light up.

You'll think so, too. Every day, people around you do good things. Most of those people don't work for you; in fact, most of them have no relationship with you, professional or personal. Compliment them for something they would least expect.

Expected feels good. Unexpected makes an even bigger impact.

Complimenting people who try something different can also be hard. Do it anyway. Status quo is often status safe. Taking a risk, however small, is hard, especially if you're insecure. Insecurity feeds off silence, so mention when you see someone trying something different. Compliment the effort. Praise the risk. Even if what they try doesn't work, they will know you noticed, and everyone likes to be noticed. And they'll know, regardless of how it turns out, that you respect them for trying.

Most of all, make the compliment personal. Compliment what the person did to achieve a certain outcome, not the outcome itself. And never be afraid to ask for help, because the act of asking is a compliment in itself--and then gives you the chance to praise someone for his or her knowledge and skill.

Give it a try. Commit to complimenting five people today, or ten, or nearly everyone you meet.

It's not easy, but I promise you'll make the day brighter for at least a few people--and you'll learn a little something about yourself, too.

I don't know about you, but I love the spirit of that experiment and story. Let's go even further on this giving trip. In

Deepak Chopra's *Seven Spiritual Laws of Success*, where "The Law of Giving" is number TWO on the list, he explains giving very simply. I'm going to share two different passages with you.

The more you give, the more you will receive, because you will keep the abundance of the Universe circulating in your life. In fact, anything that is of value in life only multiplies when it is given. That which does not multiply through giving is neither worth giving nor worth receiving. If, through the act of giving, you feel you have lost something, then the gift is not truly given and will not cause increase. If you give grudgingly, there is no energy behind that giving.

The other passage in that section speaks a million volumes about the act of giving and receiving and its importance:

Practicing the Law of Giving is actually very simple: if you want joy, give joy to others; if you want love, learn to give love; if you want attention and appreciation, learn to give attention and appreciation; if you want material affluence, help others to become materially affluent. In fact, the easiest way to get what you want is to help others get what they want. This principle works equally well for individuals, corporations, societies, and nations. If you want to be blessed with all the good things in life, learn to silently bless everyone with all the good things in life.

Okay, so check this out. Five years ago, I was working for an affiliate company out of Burleson, Texas, doing their online marketing and writing their blog posts because that is one of my day jobs when I'm not playing or writing music. The company flew everyone out for a five-day retreat at this beautiful, luxurious, Texan ranch in the middle of nowhere. Like, you could see rattlesnakes and herd cows and do Texas things, but we were mainly out there for teambuilding activities. It was one of the best experiences of my life. While I was there, I was blown away by how giving and loving this company I got to work for was. They were so good to their employees.

When I arrived at the airport after this fabulous, 'treated like rock stars' weekend, I was still on a life high. I was in line at Starbucks at the Dallas airport after having gone through security. There was a gentleman behind me, and I instinctually said to the cashier/barista, "I'll take care of whatever this gentleman is having also." He was gracious and accepted my "pay it forward" gift. I told him to have a wonderful day and headed to my gate.

Ten minutes later, this man approached me at my gate (he

had been scouring the airport looking for me). He approached me and thanked me for being so kind, then proceeded to ask me what kind of phone I was using. I let him know I am an Apple girl. He handed me his card and told me he is the Vice President of Samsung United States. THE VP OF SAMSUNG USA WAS WHO I JUST BOUGHT COFFEE FOR!!! He then told me to email him my address, because he wanted to send me the brand-new Galaxy to have. Three weeks later, I had the latest model of this company's phone for the price of a cup of coffee. But this story gets better.

When I was in college, I had amazing professors. One of them lives in Ft. Worth and I was able to see him on my trip to Texas. He also happens to use Samsung phones. He didn't know about my story with the VP of Samsung. He texted me and told me he had just shattered his cellphone. He dropped it during a photoshoot (he is a great photographer as well). What did I do? I got his address and immediately sent him the phone that had been sent to me. The Universe gave me those moments to end up helping someone else. THAT is the shit I live for. And it's not exclusive to me.

The Universe has a much bigger plan when things go haywire. The Universe provided for me and provided for my former professor. It was a beautiful thing. The Universe CONTINUES to provide for me, but I know that is because I live in a state of giving.

It's not about getting back. I know at the end of the day, that's what's going to happen. That's the Law of Attraction, and that's how awesome all of this is. Also, all timing is perfect timing. If you lose your job or lose a lover, there are no mistakes in the Universe's schedule, even though we may not feel it at the time.

Suggestions:

1. Today, as you go about your day, think about what you can give. Start by thanking the Universe for all you have. Give thanks for fresh water, food to feed your body, a warm place to lay your head, or whatever it is you're grateful for. Sit in those moments and feel that gratefulness in your body. Watch as it feels great and full...*great-ful.*

2. Consider giving an hour of your time if you don't have money. Give it to your friends or your kids. Make one phone call to make someone feel good. Pick a flower for someone. It doesn't have to be a huge gesture, or it can be. The point is to do it.

3. Go about your day in a giving Spirit. See the changes that take place in other lives and YOUR life because of your actions and attitude. You never know when an unselfish act from you can change the day or life of another human being.

9. *Ask People What They Need – Here Is an Opportunity to Serve*

Speaking of giving, asking others what you can do for them, or finding out what their needs are is a great opportunity to serve. Again, when we're serving or giving without expecting anything in return, it brings out all the feel-goods, not to mention the cosmic side effects of awesome. These need not be grandiose gestures either. As I said earlier, it could be a little something like phoning someone on your way to see him or her and asking if they need anything while you're out. It could be as simple as making dinner for someone or volunteering. Hell, buy someone a coffee. Give to a GoFundMe account for someone in need.

For as long as I can remember, I've always been a server. That wasn't a humblebrag. Serving is just a thing I do because I love to provide an environment where people feel comfortable and have everything they need.

For example, I was a "troubled teen," as some would say. I was in juvenile detention for most of my teenage life. I can't even count how many times. I was a little too independent for the parents to handle. However, that's what I had to go through to be the person I am today. During that time, I had a mentor from my church named Amber Bennington. She would come over to my home and kick it with me. I always wanted to make sure she had everything she needed. I wanted her to be comfortable and happy. Amber is the first person who ever noticed this about me and said something to me. She told me that she loved how accommodating I was with her all the time and how she saw my serving spirit. That small compliment has stayed with me since that day. Yes. I love to serve. Come to dinner at my place (once I get settled), and trust me, you'll be happy you did. I want to make people feel good. That's a thing with me. So when you ask others what they need and serve others, damn it makes you feel good because it takes the focus off of you.

I bet each and every one of you has something that makes you feel good when you do it. We are all made to serve. If you think about it, this incredible Universe we live in serves us personally every day. Not a day goes by where the Universe is not serving you air, water, or food. For those who have a hard time purchasing food, it doesn't take much to help others by giving some food items to a food pantry for those who are in need.

I also see service in the act of getting out of someone else's way, whether they are in a hurry on the road or in the grocery store. How many times have you decided to be a dick to the person in the driving lane next to you because you thought they were in too big of a hurry? I've been totally guilty of this. I've not let people over in my lane and just been a complete asshole on the road. I'm ashamed to admit it, but I have, and those actions were a part of my growth.

I refuse to behave that way today. I now get the hell out of the way and make it a priority to serve other drivers without them even knowing it. It doesn't take much on your end, just a little awareness and a little courtesy.

A quality of my ex, is that no matter what, wherever he was, he would always phone me to see if I needed anything while he was out. Did I need a coffee, or did I need something picked up from the store on his way home? Maybe, maybe not, but I always got that courtesy call, which is now something I make it a point to do. If you're going to pick up a habit, that's an excellent one to choose, and it's another form of giving.

Today and moving forward, I encourage you to make a phone call to someone, anyone, to see how you can serve them. I bet you'll feel terrific about it, PLUS, cosmic shit will align with you.

Suggestions:

1. Step outside of yourself today and ask someone how you can serve them, even if it inconveniences you. When you serve with a grateful, appreciative heart, the Universe takes note.

2. When driving to work, home from work, to the store, to get your kids, be considerate of other people who are driving alongside you.

Be the patient one. Sit back. Being courteous to others, who may not be in the same headspace as you, can work magic on your soul, and perhaps you're the reason an accident didn't happen.

3. When you serve, you will be served in return. Your service may be able to be a positive influence on someone else. So, why would you not want that?

10. Gratitude Fucking Owns

There is nothing better than starting and ending your day by saying "Thank you" to the Universe. It sets the tone for your entire day. It sets the tone for your whole life. The first moments of every day that I get to sleep in a bed, under a roof, have clean water to drink, food in the fridge, and eyes to see and ears to hear and legs to walk . . . holy fucking hell . . . I am grateful. So, when you wake up every day, gratitude is the power to see what blessings you have. There are so many out in the world who are in much worse places than you or I could ever imagine. I mean, I'm rich because I get to sit on a toilet, with water to flush, use toilet paper AND baby wipes to wipe my ass.

I am so blessed, and so are you. Many people continuously think about and work for the things they don't have, because of a society that tells us we need more to be complete and whole. Well, we are all whole right now. Your thoughts create your world. I get overwhelmed with emotion at times when I think about where I am. I don't even have my own home right now, and I'm blown away by the contentment and trust I have that everything is going to be okay. I break down in tears (man, I'm sappy as fuck, I tell you) when I listen to the album I just got to be a part of. Having gratitude evokes having my mind blown over and over, and it's fucking amazing.

Where you are in life makes you who you are. You can choose to be a bitter, unhappy person who blames your lot in life on others, or you can take responsibility for the decisions you've made to get you where you are. If you want to change, even if it's scary as hell, do the things necessary to make that change. Go to that gym, sign up for that class, let go of the fuckers and suckers in your life, move to that new city. Hell, I just moved across the country to build a new life. Do whatever it is you need to do to get your shit together. Break up with the loser lover who holds you back, quit letting others emotionally abuse you, quit being abusive to yourself, STOP being a victim. Be grateful that you have a choice. YOU get to take charge of your life.

Life is a trip most of the time, and the curveballs DO NOT have to knock you down. Even if they do, getting back up and back in the game is what matters.

I've had an amazing year, but it's been challenging at times. I've been around some unhealthy people that have broken my heart, people I have grown to love and trust who haven't been good for me. I've had to walk away from many of them. However, I wouldn't change a thing because I'm eternally grateful for the things I've learned in the past few years. I've learned so much about love, forgiveness, grace, and acceptance. I learned I am much stronger than I knew, especially when it came to making a better me. A better me affects everyone in my life. A better you affects everyone in your life. And an INSPIRED us, can help change the world.

I know from the bottom of my heart that I want to inspire change within myself and change in other people, and one of the things that sparks change is gratitude. When you find yourself in a place where you're making excuses for yourself or complaining, catch those moments. You can change your state of mind in one moment by turning your state of contempt into a state of gratitude. After all, gratitude fucking owns.

Suggestions:

1. Spend a few moments today in silent gratitude. Write down a few things you're grateful for. Try doing this in the morning to get your day started well. If you continually make this a habit, your mindset truly changes for the better, and when you change your mind, you change your life.

2. Throughout your day, give little thanks for the small victories and awesomeness that happens to you or for you. Go even as far as to reach out to someone and thank the person for helping you with something you needed help with. Your appreciation will go a long way. (And it's an open invitation to more acts of receiving.)

3. Every night before you go to bed, go through the events of your day. Be in a state of gratitude for what you DO have. You probably have a bed to sleep in, a safe space to rest, and people around you who are encouraging you throughout your life.

11. Don't Make Small Talk – Get Really Fucking Real with Your Source

Jesus ain't at the wheel. YOU are. So, where are you going to go? This is your life. It's brilliant if you choose it to be. It's the only one you have at this point. You are the only person in control of your future, and you can have whatever the hell you want in this physical plane when you tap into your Source. Oh, but let me tell you, I use the word "control" loosely. This is what I mean by control. If there is something you love to do, there is a way to do that. You control whether you take steps to create your reality. For example, I want to be a great bassist. I am in control of whether or not I rehearse daily. I want to have a New York Times Bestselling book. I am in control of whether I write a book or not. So, while the Universe has our backs when we get in the flow, it notices the actions you take daily. When you are living your truth, epic shit aligns for real. I hope you're starting to get that message, and you begin seeing how cosmic and amazing you truly are. And while we may have a plan, it's also our job to give it to the Universe, let it go, and let our Source do its thing.

In prayer, when you're communicating with your Source, I encourage you not to make small talk. Get to the nitty-gritty—the most real of real. Go to the place where you seek refuge and serenity and answers when you sit in silence. This is an essential aspect of getting out of your way. There is a magical power inside of you that is ONLY accessible through a higher power, YOUR higher self that is YOU. And it takes getting real with who YOU are, what YOU want, what YOUR vision is, and then letting go so the UNIVERSE can create the opportunities along the way.

Another thing you should remember when we're speaking with our higher power, or whatever you want to call it, there is ZERO judgment. So, it's okay to be honest because, in reality, you are honest with yourself.

How many times have you been dishonest with yourself? You may be thinking, "I don't fucking lie to myself." But hear me out; How many times have you agreed to do something you didn't want to do? How many times have you talked yourself out of doing the thing you wanted to do because you were afraid of what others may think? How many times do you ignore that nudge in your heart of hearts because you don't believe you are capable? How many times have you stayed a little too long in a shitty relationship out of fear? These, my friends, are examples of you lying to yourself.

Remember, when you get real with yourself, you're getting real with the Universe, because you and the Universe are one being and nonbeing, if that makes sense. And by the way, no one needs to know your deep thoughts. You don't have to "share" any of this with anyone, because this is YOUR shit, not theirs. It's also okay to admit you're scared, or insecure, or pissed, and have been living in those negative feelings. But this is about you, not anyone else.

The bottom line is if you no longer want to be a victim of these emotions, you must first acknowledge each emotion to change it. It's like the beginning of any 12-step program; we must first admit there's a problem. Ingrained, unhealthy ways of thinking and being are both problems. They are just as damaging to your health as any overuse of drugs or alcohol. We become addicted to the way we feel, even though the feelings don't desirably serve us, but again, it's those old habits we must break.

Some of the personal things I've dealt with, as recently as fucking today, are fear, anxiety, and lack of trust. I know that all of these emotions stem from one issue in my life. It begins with me making a significant change (which isn't THAT big). I simply have to choose a different thought, one that serves my highest self, rather than the one(s) that do not serve my highest self.

Dr. Dyer magically describes changing your thoughts to serve you:

> First, be the observer, and then the contemplator. Now become the choice maker who can consciously decide to put that thought back into the running stream (of endless

thoughts) and pick a different one, a thought that perhaps allows you to feel better.

It's like a vacuum effect: In order to let a new emotion infiltrate our lives, such as joy, love, trust, or abundance, we must let go of the old feelings that have been keeping us stuck. To get a grasp on what you want in your future, you must examine your old ways of thinking. You must surrender them to the Infinite Source, who created you with love, admiration, and intention, and then trust in the Source that it's going to show up in a way you've never imagined, in perfect timing. Trust me, the Universe loves to do that shit. And then the joy you feel from the pure KNOWING that the Universe has your back when you live in love rather than in fear, as Gabrielle Bernstein wrote about in her book, *The Universe Has Your Back*, can be outwardly celebrated.

Something else to consider, as you're getting fucking real with your Source, is this; Act as if it is so, then it will be. FEEL it in your bones and in your soul, this realness of whatever you desire as it is already so. Then it will be. And know it will be better than your mind, or my mind, could have ever imagined. Your job is not to know the how. Your job is to know, to trust, and to be.

I'm going to drive this nail in. Make meditation a daily practice. If this is your first go at it, please go back to the meditation section and see how you can begin this beautiful, ABSOLUTELY necessary aspect to your spiritual journey. Get it. Follow it. Do it. And don't waste any time. After all, this is YOUR future we're talking about here. It is imperative to connect with your Source.

While we're talking about not making small talk with your Source, let's talk about your interactions with people close to you. If you know me at all, I tend to get a little preachy sometimes. I'm just one of those people who doesn't make small talk with people. The fucks are zero when it comes to the weather, what a co-worker is doing, or what people have to bitch about. I like to jump the gun and get onto what a person is doing to reach their most meaningful goals for themselves. I wouldn't say I'm preachy, more like, coachy. I just want people to see the power they have within themselves. More often than not, it's a lot for people to handle.

At the heart of things, I feel like it's so important to have people in your corner who are going to encourage you to live to your highest potential. It's essential to have people who are going to challenge you to expand your perception of things gently. I'm attempting to do this in the book that you're reading. That just can't happen by dicking around talking about things that don't matter, ya know? I mean, sure, we can talk Colts and Packers all day long, but when it gets down to the nitty-gritty, I'm here to serve and so are you. One way to do it is by being real and loving to the people in our lives. And then, know when to shut the fuck up and just be. Be loving, be accepting, and be in the moment.

Suggestions:

1. Be completely yourself when you're sharing your desires with the Universe. If you have some baggage, you need to unload it, go for it, but then let it go. It's high time you get on living the life you truly want, and you can only get there by digging deep into yourself.

2. Remember that YOU have complete control over which voices in your head you choose to listen to. If you have a thought that is not serving your highest self, let it go and choose a different one that does. It's as simple as that.

3. Be a ray of light in someone else's life. Share your wisdom, be real with other people, but also know when to just be. The people around you will appreciate you, and your love and compassion for them. It's about finding a delicate balance.

12. *Say Yes More– Especially If It Scares the Shit Out of You*

You all know that saying, "Do something every day that scares you." If you're in the majority of the population out there, you love staying in your comfort zone. Or you could be like Marc Maron in his Netflix comedy special, Too Real, and be like, "My comfort zone is getting uncomfortable." I truly appreciate that sentiment.

I get it. Most people think comfort zones are safe. But are they? I think this idea of a comfort zone is a myth. I'm not sure where along this journey, we just decided to live safely, or ordinarily, or adopt an "it's too risky to take a chance" attitude, when we were created to be extraordinary. And I'm not sure where along the path of life we decided to let other people have input on what was good or bad for us. I think it's time we reevaluate this comfort zone bullshit business.

What if we flipped the script and decided to look at comfort zones as NOT safe? What if we looked around us and inside of our souls and thought, "Uh-oh, been in this same predicament a little too long, time to shake some shit up." Do you think it'd be easier to accept change and evolve faster?

Evolution has never come without risk, and it certainly doesn't come without change. I often think about Pulitzer Prize-winning historian Laurel Thatcher Ulrich and her famous saying,

"Well behaved women seldom make history," when I think of evolving outside of our comfort zones.

Let's say there's something you would love to do but would consider passing on it if given the opportunity because you don't think you can do it. Or you're scared. Perhaps you have all this hesitation because of your "What will people think of me?" mindset or, "What if I fail and look ridiculous?" I'm just going to go ahead and call you on your bullshit now. There are no excuses when it comes to living an incredible life!

I have had many things in my life that I could have said "no" to, but every "no" would have been a fear-based "no." And I can't get down with that. Thankfully I was born with something inside of me that wants to do everything...all of it. I think you probably were too. Maybe you just didn't have the nudge you needed, so I genuinely hope this helps.

There are a couple of real-life things I said "yes" to that changed my life even though I was scared, sooooooo scared. But seriously, looking back on everything now, this is the stuff that comes up, and then you see how one thing leads to another, because the Universe only knows the way of perfect orchestration. Let's use one of my many stories as an example.

First off, I was asked to sit on a panel for a tech conference that is held every year in Bloomington IN, called Indiana Combine.

At the time, I was a blog writer and owned my own online marketing company, which wasn't too techy (like I wasn't building apps or platforms or anything like that). Being in the world of ghost blogging and online marketing, I went ahead and said yes. From being on that panel, I was asked to give a TEDx talk about a nonprofit I co-founded called Girls Rock! Indianapolis. This was a big deal. When Christian Long, Co-Founder of WONDER, By Design, a school design studio, approached me and asked to be one of the speakers at a TEDx Bloomington entitled, "The Wisdom of Play," there was simply no way I could say no. At the time, Girls Rock! Indianapolis was one of the biggest things I was a part of. It's still growing and thriving to this day. If you're not aware of the Girls Rock programs, which are in MANY states, let me tell you about it.

Girls Rock! Indianapolis is a week-long, nonprofit summer camp for girls ages 8-16. This is a camp that empowers young girls by teaching them how to play an instrument, form a band, write a song, and then perform it in front of an always sold-out audience. Girls Rock teaches campers how to have positive self-esteem and body image, and uses music as a platform for empowerment. The campers name their own bands, they make their own logos, create their own t-shirt designs, and some learn how to play instruments from scratch. It's such a brilliant program for young girls to have space where they can be themselves and not have pressures from the opposite sex. And yes, boys rock too. I'm honored to have been a part of the creation of this in Indianapolis, alongside bandmates and good friends. I was able to talk about this program in front of hundreds of people. From that talk, I gave ANOTHER TEDx talk on the subject. Both can be viewed on YouTube if you want to check them out. Those two talks were kind of an "icing on the cake" deciding factor in my getting hired to play bass for my dream band by my current boss (the singer of the group I'm in).

When Cold asked me to be a part of their band, THAT was scary for me. A dream come true alert? I mean, how often do people get THOSE calls? I could have easily said, "No, I'm not good enough." Hell no! I thought of the Richard Branson quote at THAT moment, "If somebody offers you an amazing opportunity, but you are not sure you can do it, say yes – then learn how to do it later!" That's what I did. I spent months and ended up getting a couple of years learning and preparing their songs. I became an all-around better bassist because I was playing my instrument a lot more.

If you have an opportunity appear in front of you, there is a reason. Work through your fear and turn it into a growing lesson that the Universe put in your life. I am now a better bassist, a better writer, and an all-around better musician because of this opportunity. I worked, I practiced, I put in the time. I am now a member of a fantastic band, and just got to record their sixth studio album with them. Additionally, I know that my life has changed because of this. And who knows, maybe it all started with that first TEDx talk that started because of Indiana Combine, that happened because of being a ghostwriter, that happened because I moved to Indianapolis, that happened because of my divorce…You get the point. All VERY scary things to do.

That being said, let's talk about public speaking for a second because doing a TED talk is nerve-wracking as hell. Public speaking scares the living piss out of me. I get crazy nervous (like, diarrhea nervous) getting up in front of people and speaking, which is funny because I can play music all day long and sing for you, but public speaking is downright hell for me. However, it's all about taking risks. Mark Zuckerberg, founder of Facebook, said it best: "The biggest risk is not taking any risk… In a world that's changing quickly, the only strategy that is guaranteed to fail is not taking risks." In other words, and these are MY words, that's saying, "Don't be a pussy, and get out of that comfort zone."

If you think about it, when you say yes, the only thing that's left for you to do is to PREPARE. Make a plan of action. Make a list. Start an outline. Ask for wisdom and guidance from your Source and just start. Preparation is the key to success in presentations. Well, and passion. Luckily, I had all the passion in the world about the subject of Girls Rock Indy, so I was able to deliver a passionate message in front of hundreds of people. I did it. I pulled it off, and out of that, I have made lifelong friends who've made lasting impressions on me. All GOOD things.

Always keep in mind, life passes you by when you say no out of fear. So I say, say yes more often. I mean, unless it's something you genuinely don't want to do, then no is totally okay. Just make sure you're deciding for the right reasons.

Suggestions:

1. Think about the opportunities you have in your life right now. How are you handling them? Do you tend to say "no" to things that are outside of your comfort zone? I implore you to look inside yourself and ask the hard questions.

2. Take one day this week and try something new. Try a new class at the gym. Try rock climbing at your local rock-climbing spot with instructors (and safety harnesses!). Maybe take a chance to hang out with someone new. Go to a new restaurant. ANYTHING. Just try something new that you've never done before.

3. Remember that you're fucking awesome. Give yourself all the credit in the world for being more than capable of making some amazing shifts happen in your life. You got this!

13. It's Okay to Let Down Your Guard Sometimes

Letting down your guard and opening up your heart can be challenging. I understand this. It means to TRUST, and it also means to HOPE. A lot of times, people can suck, but most of the time, people are good. As you continue to grow into a more conscious person, you will be able to easily recognize who and what is good for you as you evolve. Also, the more you trust and know who you are inside, the more the quality of people who show up in your world magically changes. Regardless, every person comes into your life for a reason.

Sometimes letting down your guard is as simple as saying "yes," as we talked about in the previous chapter. Perhaps it's as simple as you letting go of judgments you've placed on yourself, other people, or external situations that you have no control over. Sometimes it's being kind to someone who has hurt you. Sometimes it's forgiving someone who has hurt you and giving them another chance.

No matter what it is, having a hard heart is not something any of us want to walk around with. How good does that feel? It feels shitty, to be honest. The best thing we can do for our hearts and our health is to be vulnerable. Be open to what is to come because it is SUPPOSED to happen to you and for you. It's about trusting in the

Universe.

There are lessons in letting down your guard. I mean, I think you want to be a badass, not a hard ass. On the other hand, it's okay to say "No" to some people in order to protect your heart, as you interact with them more and learn what their true intentions are. It's okay to walk the fuck away.

There was once someone in my life that I considered a best friend. This person was much younger than me, so I consistently gave them "passes" for their immature, often narcissistic behavior. Time and time again, I would have issues with behavior and vent to close friends (which is not something I recommend because by doing that, I was asking the Universe to give me more bullshit that was of the same nature. I know this now.) Time and time again, I would still want to give the person love. I would try to be there, give more chances, and each time, I would be betrayed in some way or another. I was finally done. After years of being hurt, I decided I no longer wanted to associate with that person. And I cried a lot. The good news is, I learned so much about myself, and that I am a good friend. I appreciate the good times we had, and I'm 1000% okay with my decision.

There are times in my life when I think about people who've hurt me, who've said mean and terrible things to me or about me. In these moments of feelings that I'm now able to be conscious of, I turn my hurt into silent blessings for those individuals. It's a way for me to turn my pain into positive, loving energy because that's genuinely the only thing I want to have surrounding me. That is my focus.

Know your balance, and while it is important to be vulnerable, don't let people walk all over you. Speaking of not letting people walk all over you, I used to have recurring nightmares about vampires, and now I get why. I would allow people to literally suck the life out of me. You know those people who only talk about themselves, who take and take and take and never give, who always need the attention and get pissy or irritable when it's not on them, gross. Walk away. And if you happen to be one of those people, it's time to get real about what the fuck is up.

There is a HUGE difference between loving who you are, being in Spirit to be a better person and, being completely self-absorbed in everything you do and throwing a fit when things aren't to your liking. A saying that is of importance to me, that is on my bulletin board from Dr. Wayne Dyer says, "My life is bigger than I am." This means that this shit isn't all about me or you. Many people are affected by the way you treat them, and if people treat you badly, take that as a big fat sign from the Universe. That's why you get those people the fuck out of your productive life. You know the saying, "Birds of a feather flock together." It's true. If you're one of those people, please stop. That's why cool people who may *care* about you aren't around…because they don't necessarily *like* you.

Don't be the person who calls your friends only when you need something. And don't only talk about the things you're going through without asking the recipient of your story how their day was or what's going on in their life.

In my own life, I am fully aware that there have been times when things are going "good" or if I have a boyfriend that I'm super into, I've fallen off the face of the planet. I don't call or text my friends as often when I'm in a relationship. That's something I'm working on as a person. I guess it takes being aware, being conscious of what's going on around you. Come to terms, forgive yourself, own your shit, and make an effort to be a better person.

Suggestions:

1. Take some time and think about the people or situations in your life that you currently have your guard up around. While it's essential to protect yourself, it's also important to be open to evolution. How can you be in this situation? How are you judging it? Consider letting it go and just being.

2. Examine your behavior in life. Are you a good friend? Are you a

good listener? Or do you make everything about you? If you have in the past, because I know we ALL have, forgive yourself, make amends where you need, and start over at this moment right now.

3. Walk away from the vampires. If you don't have people in your life encouraging you to be a better person or you have people in your life who discourage you, let them go. Once you do, the right people will show up in your life.

14. *Fuck Everyone Else's Opinions*

Heed the following saying, "Opinions are like assholes. Everyone has one and they typically stink." Everyone has a right to their opinion, but remember it is only their opinion and should not be taken as the gospel by you. If it does not fit the view that you have for yourself, then leave it and go your own way.

You have this thing or things to do in life. We all have a purpose, whether we adhere to it or not. It is my hope with this book that you find your passion and go with it. When you get inspired to do something, and begin doing the work towards whatever the hell it is you're passionate about, people will always have something to say. DO NOT LISTEN TO ANYONE. One of the greatest things ever written by Dr. Wayne Dyer in his book, *Living an Inspired Life* was:

> Suffering the consequences of living according to someone else's wishes doesn't make any sense; rather, we need to oppose the external opinions that try to force us to be what we're not intended to be.

People may disapprove but I promise, if you remain steadfast, they will begin to accept and respect you. You're getting to the root of what you need to get done on this earth. You're working toward fulfilling YOUR calling, not your family's or your friends' calling for you. They may even be asserting what they feel is in your best interest. As Abraham Maslow famously stated, "Be independent of the good opinions of others."

Here's a little example of what I mean. When I was a young child, I knew I wanted to be a "rock star." In other words, I wanted to make a living playing music because it was (and still is) one of the most important aspects of who I am. I would spend countless hours in front of a mirror with an upright vacuum and sing my heart out to Courtney Love, Eddie Vedder, Billy Corgan, or whatever band I was obsessed with at the time. I eventually picked up a guitar and realized how much I loved creating music and writing songs. And how simple it was, and how it came to me easily. However, I got so much resistance from my family. They would say things like, "You have to KNOW people," or "Do you know how hard it is to succeed in the music industry?" or, "That's impossible."

Every time I heard any of these things, I thought quietly to myself, "Well then, I'll get to know as many people as I can in the music industry, and I'll work to create the best music I can." Then I would think of some song that was currently in radio rotation and believe that if that song could make it, mine could too. I now have a song I wrote as the intro and outro music to the popular *Fitfluential Radio* podcast and have been a guest on the podcast as well. As a child and throughout adulthood, I've overcome a lot of bullshit and a lot of discouragement.

So, what was in my power personally to make this dream of mine come true? I continued to write songs, sing, and perform at coffee house open mic nights. I hung out with other musicians and would collaborate and write songs with them. I went to concerts. I started knocking on bus doors. I began making friends who were musicians and met leaders in the music industry. I intended to someday work with the people I met in the music industry, so I wanted to create relationships and gain respect. I went all in.

I still remember the four-hour drive one random night to see the band, Incubus, before they were a huge band selling out stadiums, at a small venue in Columbus, Ohio. I was OBSESSED with their cassette, S.C.I.E.N.C.E., and it's the only thing I would listen to for three months straight.

My best girlfriend and I arrived at the venue early, so I went right up to their bus, knocked on the door, and said, "We just drove four hours to come to your show because we love your work." That night ended up being magical. Singer and all-around badass, Brandon Boyd, hung out with me graciously, and we went for a walk around that neighborhood in Columbus, which was only a couple of blocks. We had a great conversation and hung out that evening after the show. The set of balls I had knocking on that door and laying it out there led to many nights of backstage passes and incredible shows all over the country, if they were near where I was living at the time. I still have to give it up to the Incubus guys, especially Mike Einziger, for always hooking it up. I did something that scared me, and it paid off. I still remember my heart pounding as I knocked on their bus door.

Nearly twenty-five years later, as a result of working hard in the music industry, I am living my dream of playing with musicians of this caliber. This shit does not come overnight. The musicians who "make it" out of nowhere, have worked their ASSES off for years, sometimes decades, before you even know their names. Hell, many people don't know my name, nor will ever know my name, and I'm cool with that because I'm doing what I love. That's all that matters.

No matter what your dream is, you have to see it, breathe it, and believe in it. Dr. Wayne Dyer has an incredible book entitled, *You'll See It When You Believe It.* It couldn't' be truer. Dr. Dyer also touches on following YOUR path despite what other people say, in his book, *I Can See Clearly Now.* There are three passages from this book I'm going to share to drive in this point on a VERY spiritual level because your passion hopefully goes beyond ego.

From a distance I can see the truth in the idea that when I follow my excitement, I align myself with the *I am* as an infinite being. The excitement or feeling of inner bliss that arises when I contemplate what I truly know I must do is God-realization. When I stay in that state of following my bliss, everything I undertake is not only going to be effortless, but even more significantly, I will be fully supported by the universe.

He goes on to say, "I discovered that when I follow my excitement, it is akin to turning the entire project over to God and watching the endless flow of synchronistic miracles unfold perfectly." And finally, this is what I feel is the most important regarding this chapter. He shares, "Sharpen your insight and be willing to trust that what you are feeling inside is what you should be doing, regardless of what everything and everyone around you might be saying to the contrary."

I always get so inspired during award season, hearing the speeches of those who win Grammys, Emmys, Golden Globes, and Tonys. While the road to where you want to be can be tricky, and it will be tricky if that's what you believe, almost everyone who wins such esteemed awards factor in that there is some higher power at play, and they never gave up because their art was in their heart. It DROVE them. This passion and faith are two of the most important things in creating your reality.

When the band, Twenty One Pilots, won their Grammy for Best Pop Duo / Group Performance in 2017, their acceptance speech in their underwear made me cry my face off out of awe and inspiration. So, to quote singer Tyler Joseph, "Anyone, from anywhere, can do anything." Always remember that. They are inspirational examples of never giving up. Just a few years before they won the award, no one had heard much about them, as they were hanging around in their underwear watching the Grammys on television.

It doesn't matter what your dream is, get it. Had I listened to what anyone said to me, I would not be living my dream, and I would not be going with my calling. I am a musician, but I am also a FAN. I am a writer, but I also love to READ. I love creating, and I am so blessed to be able to give lifelong memories and positive experiences to fans and readers, because some of the experiences I had kept me on the right track.

Suggestions:

1. Follow your bliss. Remember the words of Dr. Dyer; "Sharpen your insight and be willing to trust that what you are feeling inside is what you should be doing, regardless of what everything and everyone around you might be saying to the contrary."

2. Remember that it's okay to fail or to fall. A child learning how to walk, never said after he or she fell, "This isn't for me." We all got up and kept going on. We learn most from our failures.

3. Remember that when you're connected with the Source, ALL things are possible. Put your dream out there and work daily to achieve it. Believe in yourself because, in that belief, you believe in God, since we are one and the same.

15. Fuck Expectations – Create Your Own Normal

In the same vein as "Fuck everyone else's opinions" it's also perfectly okay to say, "Fuck off." to other people's expectations of you as well. This particular little piece of advice is essential to me. You see, I don't do things in a normal manner. I never have. Ever since I was a little kid, my parents would say white, and I'd fall in love with black. My dad would root for the Detroit Lions, and I'd root for whatever team was playing against them. I'm not sure why my little mind always wanted to go against the grain of everything and everyone, including my own family. I guess I just needed to find some kind of place for independence. I still do. That's why I believe that this book, which is based upon the Law of Attraction and spirituality yet has the word "fuck" in the title, is going to be just fine. I am always going against the grain and still creating my own normal.

I'm also a mother. I am blessed to have an amazing, sixteen year-old daughter who is the kindest, most creative, most loving, little girl on the planet. She also doesn't live with me. She's with me as much as she can be, but she lives full time with her amazing father. He and I have the most beautiful friendship and relationship.

So, how could I be a mother and not live with my child? I'll tell you that story. I was in love with my daughter's father at one point in my life. I met him at a tattoo shop when I was eighteen years old when I went with one of my girlfriends to get a body piercing. He was the body piercer, no less. I was so enamored with him at the time. He was tattooed, good looking, seemed confidant, was intelligent, loved music, had a job, etc. He made such an impact on me that I went and got my tongue pierced the following day by him and went out with him the next weekend. There was chemistry.

We started dating regularly. I wanted to spend all of my time with him and get to know him. So, I managed to convince him to let me be his body-piercing apprentice. I was super into tattoos, loved body modification anyway (I pierced my nose when I was fourteen), and I also wanted to find a trade I enjoyed because college was not on my priority list at the time. He agreed. I spent the next nine months in the tattoo shop where I learned the trade I would use for the next four years of my life. Keep in mind, I was also still very much into music, so this was a step that made sense in that I wanted to do something where I could make my schedule, make good money, and still work on my musical endeavors.

Over those nine months, I moved in with this guy, had a passionate yet tumultuous relationship, and he ended up breaking my heart. I had to get out of the place I grew up in to find my way. I packed up and moved, for the first time in my life, to another city.

Fast forward a few years. I found myself living in Tampa,

Florida, and asked him to move down. I was in a band that was playing weekends, and I needed a reliable piercer who could take on the volume of clients at the Ybor City tattoo shop I worked in. Naturally, we became an item again. We tried to make it work. Nope, it didn't. So he moved to Chicago to go to art school. Then for some reason, I moved up to Chicago to try to make it work AGAIN. When it didn't work, because we really couldn't get on the same page, I found myself back in my hometown of Kokomo, IN. We weren't even together as a couple when I got pregnant. It was just a hookup. So, we decided to commit to being great parents, and being okay with us not being together.

After our daughter was born, we did try to give it a go again, but by then we were both mature enough to realize it just wasn't happening. We were not meant to be together as a couple. I see now that we were always meant to be great, supportive parents that hold one another up in all circumstances. Not only do we win, but our daughter wins. If we're alright, she knows she's alright.

When I first moved away from my daughter, there were people in my life who judged me, and did not approve of her father taking the role of primary caregiver. I had sole custody of her, and she was five years old at the time. I was going through a divorce, and needed to take the next steps in order to help provide for her. I had just received my bachelor's degree, and the move I needed to make was away from any support system. I just needed to get away from the dreary little town I had waited to escape my whole life only to find myself back there and miserable. She was in a more stable environment with her father, and I was smart enough to understand that. I wanted what was best for us all. And quite frankly, her father having that responsibility was just as important for him. It really made him step up to be the amazing man and father he is today.

We're still close, still best friends, always there for one another, always share holiday time with my family, and no one can take that away from us. I adore his wife who has been an amazing stepmother, (they are currently separated), and they have a child together whom I love as much. We don't fight over weekends or time. When I want her to come to California, we put her ass on a plane. When we need to pay for stuff, we talk to each other and make it work. No courts involved. When you can make your relationship with the person whom you share a child with not about YOU, life can be incredible. We live this reality daily. I even stay with them when I go back to Indiana.

It pains me to hear stories about completely selfish parents who put children in the middle of their bullshit. That is fucking toxic, and if you're doing that, you need to grow up. Not only do YOU suffer, but the children also suffer. We need to raise healthy, loving, accepting, and kind children to make change in this world. That shit starts with you. So, do whatever it takes. If there is a jealous spouse or boy/girlfriend who can't handle that, it's time to reconsider that toxic relationship. Anyone you choose as a partner needs to be a supportive voice and have enough emotional maturity to see the bigger picture. Love is the answer here. Not fear or insecurity.

I'm incredibly grateful to the Universe. She knew what she was doing when she brought my daughter's Father into my life. We won against all the odds, and against what anyone said. It's funny because he and I sit back and giggle (mainly joke) sometimes about us now being the most functional people in our families when we used to be the most dysfunctional. May all of your parenting relationships be as rad as the one I have with Jayme.

Suggestions:

1. I had to overcome the stigma of other people saying I was "abandoning" my child. This was one of the most challenging things in my life. However, I knew better. I was doing what was best for all of us. I knew I was not abandoning her. It didn't then, nor does it now, matter what anyone else thinks. We have created our own normal, and we are all very happy and supportive of one another. I encourage you to find YOUR new normal.

2. Not everyone is going to be lucky in the supportive parent category. If this is your case, I'm so very sorry. You can't control other people, which is why you have to rely on you. You CAN control how you react to things. If you focus on the wrong things, you'll get more of that. Again, it's that damn Law of Attraction. Perhaps think about something good, and give a compliment or a word of encouragement to the person with whom you share a child. Give love/get love. Give support/get support. But expect nothing in return. Be and do from a place of love if you want to see changes in your life and the life of your child.

3. Remember to give thanks for the little steps of improvement. Give yourself a nod of encouragement when you handle a situation better than you did the week before. Be aware of how you perceive and react to certain situations. Try to be the conscious observer and thank the Universe for showing you wisdom. You got this. Plus, your kid will notice it as well.

To close this chapter up, I feel called to give you the "Prayer of Saint Francis". Perhaps this will help in dealing with issues that are difficult in all of your relationships.

Lord, make me an instrument of your peace,

Where there is hatred, let me sow love;

Where there is injury, pardon;

Where there is doubt, faith;

Where there is despair, hope;

Where there is darkness, light;

And where there is sadness, joy.

O Divine Master,

Grant, that I may not so much seek

To be consoled as to console,

To be understood, as to understand,

To be loved, as to love.

For it is in giving that we receive,

It is in pardoning that we are pardoned,

And it is in dying that we are born to Eternal Life.

16. The BEST Shit Comes Out of the Worst (When You're In the Flow)

And yes, go ahead and thank the perfection of the Universe for this. I love those little videos and photos from The Law of Attraction Instagram account that are circulating social media right now. My favorite one is the one about worry. It says:

One day, you'll look back and realize that you worried too much about things that don't really matter. And you will actually be glad things didn't work out the way you wanted them to. So stop it. Stop overthinking. You can't control everything. Just let it be. Let go of what's gone, be grateful for what remains, look forward to what's to come. Because eventually you'll end up where you need to be, with who you're meant to be with and doing what you should be doing. Have faith and hope…There is something positive and new on the horizon. You just can't see it yet. But what is meant for you will NOT pass by.

My parents just got divorced seven years ago after forty-one years together. Why? My dad fell in love with another woman. Yeah, he sucked and cheated. The irony in this story, which is laughable, is that this behavior was completely unacceptable according to my upbringing. My mom has been pretty devastated since it all happened. She's still working through her issues with it, but I have to be honest, I'm not upset with my dad all that much. I know some people think I should be, but I like his new wife, and he's in love with her, AND he's happy. Yeah, what he did was shitty and sucks, but I am a firm believer that it takes two people to fuck up a marriage. If there's infidelity, something is awry (unless the cheater is just a narcissistic asshole, in that case, let go and good riddance). But at the end of the day, communication is THE MOST important thing if you're not happy in a marriage. Hell, it's JUST as important if you ARE happy. But in this situation, I genuinely believe that the responsibility falls on both of them.

As a teenager, I felt like attention in my home was always based on the wrong things. Strong faith is good, but ignoring the reality that you're still fucking human and have human wants and needs, whether or not you live a faith-based life, is pretty naïve. I believe that's what happened to my family. There were too many rules, too much control, time at bible study, and outside obligations rather than communicating and doing things together, taking care of the needs of one another.

On the flip side of that, my mother is AMAZING and stayed faithful to my father all those years. But she wasn't happy deep down inside. This unhappiness caused her to surrender to some of her demons, like overeating and not taking care of herself. She was kind of a doormat who put up with my dad being pretty selfish most of the time because well, in their faith, you don't get divorced. From a human perspective, I believe the divorce was a gift to both of them.

Through this hot mess of shit, my mother got a second chance to do something for HER. She stood by my dad as he went through school, changed careers, umpired softball games, while she took care of three WONDERFUL kids and six grandchildren, held a job, sang in the choir at church, the list goes on and on. But she never really learned what HER passion was and what SHE loved to do because she built her entire world around other people.

The story of my parents is one of the reasons why I say in the beginning, YOU are THE most important person in your life. So many people live in this world thinking it's selfish to put themselves first, but that's all a façade. It's not selfish at all. It's selfish for you NOT to put yourself first. You can't give others something if it's missing inside of you. It is always my goal to help people find what they're passionate about, and pursue that passion because that's a calling. It is a God-given calling.

My mom now has a calling to learn what her passion is. I think she should write a book. She's a killer writer (but honestly, my opinion doesn't fucking matter). So, I guess we'll see what happens. I'm going to be here to encourage her to learn who she is. But in all of this, whenever I now think about a breakup or a relationship or situation that ended and broke my heart, I think about something my numerologist Joni says to me that I mentioned before; "You can't lose something good for you." Just as the Law of Attraction says, "What is meant for you will not pass you by." However, you have to be open and ready to receive.

I truly believe my mom has a wonderful life ahead of her, better than she ever could have imagined and better than it EVER would have been with my father, as long as she stays in alignment with love, forgiveness, and hope. Her best time is yet to come where she gets to experience the kind of happiness that she's never experienced. Her job is to keep her heart open.

She is still going through the process of forgiving and letting go. I am continually giving her things to read and encouraging her to meditate and get in tune with who she is. I am a firm believer that everything DOES happen for a reason. You have to pick yourself up when terrible things happen. Otherwise, they will kill you. Faith and patience are 1000% necessary. So please, remember that flowers bloom with no help from us after a dead winter. Trees flourish with leaves after they've been long gone. A caterpillar goes into a cocoon thinking it's dying when in fact, it's transforming. Know that good comes out of the messes that we're supposed to experience for positive transformation.

Suggestions:

1. If you're going through something that's one of the hardest things you've ever experienced, please keep the words of Betty Rocker in mind: "You've made it through 100% of your worst days." This, too, shall pass, my friends.

2. It's time to start taking responsibility for the things that are in your life. Good or bad, you attract the people and situations in your life. Even if this is not easy to hear, it's fucking real. If you want better things to show up for you, focus on being what you want. If you are in that place, and things still don't go as you want them to, then thank the Universe for knowing what you need better than you do.

3. There's a brilliant line in the song "Closing Time", by Semisonic, that I'd like you to keep in mind when a chapter of your life is closing, and a new one is beginning; "Every new beginning comes from some other beginning's end." Sometimes the one thing in life we need for us to reach a place of living as our highest selves is a new beginning.

17. *Always Be Your Authentic Self*

As I write this chapter of this book, I'm going through boxes of things at my father's house in Indiana, where I was born and raised. I'm in a weird transition phase of moving, writing, rehearsals, and embarking on my first tour with Cold.

In 1998, I decided to get out of Indiana to pursue a music career in Florida. I had heard there was a good rock scene there, so I went with my then bassist to start a new band in the city of Gainesville. While that band didn't work out, and everyone went their own way, I made some good friends. I was able to move in with a girlfriend on campus and get a job as a gas station attendant. I would've worked in a tattoo shop, but there were only a couple of tattoo shops in that town, and no one was hiring so, I did what I had to do.

At this particular gas station, we had the same customers every morning and every afternoon. I grew very fond of everyone who came in. I knew their names, their schedule, how they took their coffee, and what brand of beer they drank.

One customer in particular, was one of my favorites. His name was Michael. To this day, I don't know his last name. I don't know where he is or what he's done, but we used to drink 40s of Mickey's, smoke weed on his front porch, and talk about our dreams.

My dream was to move to Santa Monica, and be able to play music for a living. He told me he never really had any grandiose dreams. He just wanted to be happy. We never had a romantic relationship, not that I would need to justify it, I'm just giving you context. He was the shit. I can still picture his hipster beard (this was way before it was cool to have a beard), and his smile. He was a kind, gentle soul.

I was getting ready to move to St. Petersburg to stay with a good friend who was currently living there, because the music thing wasn't happening in Gainesville for me. I wasn't about to move back to Indiana at that point, so I was in my last days of working at this gas station. My buddy, Michael, came into my work with this note that I've always kept dear to my heart. I used to carry it with me everywhere, but somehow it ended up in a box that was being stored at my dad's since I've been moving so much. I just found it, so I'm going to share it with you now.

> Wish I could let you know what I see or let you know all the great things that happen when you smile or how much the honesty in your laugh means. I wish I could push a button and fix it all for ya. I can't really express how much these little things mean. But I can say thank you. The last few months of my life haven't been good either but you have cheered

things up and that's why I say thanks. Please just keep working and your eye on the prize. Yeah. Also, no matter what ever may happen, keep a small memory of me in that head of yours.

Sincerely, Michael 1/9/1999

This very short relationship and interaction happened because I was my authentic self, and he was as well. There was never anything to prove. I was always real and honest with him, which is something I strive to do daily with ALL my interactions, and he was genuine and honest about who he was with me. Now, twenty-one years later, I get to see a reminder that I helped this man as he helped me. And I have a memory of him in this head of mine.

Every day, your actions matter. It doesn't matter where you are in life. It doesn't matter if you're a gas station attendant, a bookstore clerk, a waiter, an A-list actor, a famous musician, a best-selling author, a wife, a mom, a husband; your actions matter. And who you truly are, your authentic self, can have the power to positively affect the hearts and souls of others. If you're not a nice person, well, good luck in life. Maybe this will motivate you to take a good look at yourself.

But if you're open to constant growth and evolution, and want to make a positive impact on those around you, BE THAT person daily. You'll reap the rewards. Oh, and by the way, my daughter was born on January 9, five years to the day after Michael gave me this note. Coincidence? I don't believe in that shit anymore.

Being authentic will help you in every aspect of your life. Listen to your heart every step of the way, from eliminating the unnecessary shit in your life to sharing little hopeful rays of light on your way to doing what you were born to do. Be who you are and go with what makes YOU feel good. If it doesn't make you feel good, it's not right for you. And if something or someone does make you feel good, take the time to celebrate it with gratitude.

Suggestions:

1. Remember that you're a beautiful, UNIQUE spirit, and your authentic self will get you much further than trying to live up to someone else's standards. Don't be afraid to change when and if you need to. All of us are in a constant state of growth, change, evolution, whatever you want to call it. And that's okay. Bring it!

2. No matter where you work, what you do, how you serve, remember that being light and love to others can be all the spark they need to get out of a dark spot they may be in. I didn't know my friend felt this way. We never really know what is going on in the

worlds of other people. I'm so happy he wrote this note to me, and I'm just as glad I still have it to share with you today.

3. If you feel someone else has inspired YOU, reach out. Send a note or a text. Give some feedback. Let someone know how special and influential they've been in your life. Keep the circle of positivity going.

18. *The Work You Get to Do MATTERS*

Because we just talked about being your authentic self, we need to talk about what you get to do in your life. I was at a party a couple of years ago in Hollywood. It was my first holiday party in LA at the time. What's insane about this party was that almost everyone who was there was either in writing, television, music, or music publishing. I mean, talk about hitting the fucking jackpot of super cool people, it was once again, a perfect chess play in my idea of Universal orchestration.

I met a nice woman who owns these super cool coffee stands around Los Angeles. She brews her cold brew coffee called Cold Bruja, which, in my personal opinion, tastes amazing. You can find it on Amazon. I highly recommend it, and I'm drinking it this very minute. As we were discussing our various music projects and my book project, Milana, who owns the coffee company, mentioned that she didn't feel like she was making a difference in her work. This story was all sad and brilliant all at the same time. Sad because she felt that way, but brilliant because I could let her know that what she did matters. She has an impact on hundreds of people a day. We had such an uplifting conversation that day because of her honesty with me, a stranger. She gets it now.

She changed the way she was looking at things. Her

thoughts were, "I'm not making a difference because I'm not doing things like you're doing, writing a book, or making music, or creating the stuff that others at this party were creating." She now realizes that she can change lives EACH and EVERY day through her smile and warmth during her service. SHE can turn someone's day around. It doesn't matter if you're the cashier at a retail store, a garbage collector, or any number of jobs out there in the world, when you give a smile, a kind word, or good service experience out of love for what you're doing at that moment, you and what you do, fucking matters.

I recently needed to get some papers notarized, so I went to visit a UPS store in Marina Del Rey. The girl who helped me was the kindest, most upbeat woman with the best attitude. If I had been the CEO of UPS or a secret shopper, she would've gotten a promotion on the spot. This woman, who was in her 20's, knew what it meant to serve, just by being as lovely as she could be. I walked out of that UPS store happy, excited, and pretty pumped that this woman loved her job, and loved to be of service to someone who needed help.

Be the person in love with what you do, even if you know you don't want to be doing it forever. When I was eighteen, I worked at a McDonald's drive thru. No shit, this is true. I had just gotten my apartment, and worked two jobs to help make ends meet.

So I'd wake up at 4 am, and be a part of the team to open up the restaurant. I'm not gunna lie. I loved it. I loved being able to serve people with their coffee, and be one of their first outside home interactions each morning. I wanted them to leave my drive-thru window in a better mood than when they arrived. It made me feel good to make other people feel good. It made me feel good to serve, and make someone else feel special even if it was just helping in a McDonald's drive-thru.

At one point in time, I worked at Walmart as a cashier. Again, I loved that job. I loved people walking out of my line in a happier state than when they arrived. I feel blessed with my work over the past 22 years that morphed into my dream job. No matter where I was, I always enjoyed myself as long as I was serving other people. But even more than that, I CHOSE to enjoy myself.

Let me ask you a question. Do you feel in your life, you look at the bright side of things, or are you more of a moaner and groaner, woe is me, this isn't where I want to be, kind of person? If you're the latter, I highly encourage you to think about the logic in that for a minute. Why choose to be miserable over where you currently are, or what you're now doing in your life? You're here because this is what you're choosing. If you want to do something different, by all means, make the necessary changes. If you think it's too hard, or you can't do it, then you're right. If you believe you

CAN do it, you're also right. I can't stress this enough. You are created by a loving, abundant Source who gave you EVERYTHING you need to succeed in doing whatever it is that brings your heart, soul, and life joy.

I believe joy is one of our natural states of being. And by the way, I don't think it's a coincidence that my middle name is Joy. I also know that joy can be an easy thing to get zapped away if we don't recognize what is happening in our environments. Every day, we have a choice to switch our emotions. We can change our shitty thoughts in the moments we recognize that our thoughts are about to go there or have crossed that threshold. WE have all the power in us to turn those thoughts around in EVERY area of our life.

You may not be in your dream job right now. Life isn't a race to the finish line. It's a journey, and how you decide to handle that journey has everything to do with how happy and satisfied you'll be in life no matter where you are at the time. When you choose to love every moment of it, it's magical. If you hate it, change it. Stop bitching and take action. No else will do it for you.

Suggestions:

1. Always remember that no matter where you are in life, you have a purpose in the EXACT place you're currently in. When you have

a moment where you want to complain, stop the thought in its tracks, and ask the Universe how you can serve.

2. Be aware of the power you possess to turn someone's life around for the better. You could be the reason someone chooses another day. There are things we can't even begin to comprehend about what another person goes through daily. If we can keep that in mind when we're interacting with others, it allows us to get outside of our petty, worldly judgments, and see ourselves in everyone.

3. Wake up and kick ass in whatever position you're in, in whatever city you're in, and whatever mood you happen to be in. When you can overcome your bullshit and live in a different frame of mind, every day is fucking magical. Live in the magic. It's way better than any other choice you could make.

19. You Are Not Your Job

While I just shared my thoughts in the previous chapter that what you do matters, it is also important to remember that you are YOU. You are NOT your job. For many people, what they do for their job is what defines who they think they are as a person. If something happens that we perceive as unfavorable with our job, it can have severe implications on our self-esteem. I experienced this when my old band, Neon Love Life, broke up.

NLL began our journey back in 2009 when I was going through my divorce, and all I needed was to be in music. I joined forces with some dear friends because we were also founding Girls Rock! Indianapolis.

In the beginning phases of this program, we thought nothing would be cooler than starting our own band of four women and leading by example. Neon Love Life was born, and we were one of the most popular bands in Indianapolis for years. Not only did we have a mission, but we all also had great song ideas. We were sister souls and best friends. I spent nearly all of my time with these women, and we shared incredibly unique chemistry. Also, we had friends and a community that got behind us, and helped make Girls Rock! Indianapolis what it has become today.

Neon Love Life ended up breaking up two years after our

launch. There were a multitude of factors: Ashley, our guitarist, wanted to go to Yale to become a gynecologist. She was, and still is, a significant advocate for female reproductive rights, and is a practicing physician for Planned Parenthood in Denver, Colorado. Our drummer Tasha wanted to focus on her massage practice and today has her own shop, which is one of the best ones in Indianapolis, called Lift Indy. Sharon, who shared guitar, bass, and vocal duties with me, works half the year in St. Croix and part of the year back in Indianapolis, still helping to run Girls Rock.

I would honestly say that my drive in the success of NLL threw a major wrench in the band. I kept going, going, going, and all of us weren't on the same page. The split came as a surprise to me after a few months of pent up tensions, of which I was aware. Ashley had announced her separation from the band because she had just gotten accepted to Yale. I immediately, without taking into consideration her feelings, posted on social media that we were looking for her replacement, because I wasn't about to stop this train. I offended a lot of people, including my bandmates. The girls told me we were splitting a week later. Looking back now, I would have done things differently. However, the split was bound to happen no matter what I would have done because that was what the Universe had in store for us.

I was in such a state of shock when I was confronted and told that we were disbanding. It threw me into a downward spiral of depression. I spent days in bed, crying, hurting, wondering what the fuck had just happened. For some reason, in my head, I was trying to figure out if people would still love me or like me if I wasn't a part of that group. I even asked my boyfriend at the time if he still wanted to be with me since I wasn't a part of that band, to which he said, "of course." That's how wrapped up my identity was in being a part of that band. I think I was also feeling shame. Shame that something I was so proud of and so in love with didn't work out. It was heartbreaking.

For years, I was pretty confident that I had known who I was, or thought I was. It was so easy to get caught up in the idea and dream of the little success we had achieved. I just wanted more, wanted to work harder, wanted to be better, but no one else had the same dream I had. So it ended. However, what I thought was a complete failure at the time ended up teaching me so much about myself and the taught me about people around me. It taught me that I had no control over the Universe's plan of success for me. It also made me learn that I was not what my job or band was. It made me learn how to pick myself up and begin again. It made me strive to be a better player and turned me into a better songwriter. It makes me think of the saying, "One day, you'll look back and be glad things didn't work out the way you wanted them to." I certainly wasn't in the healthiest place in my life. I was drinking a lot, and I was going out a lot. There were behaviors I needed to change, and honestly, it would take years after this event in my life for me to even get to that person I would need to become to take on true responsibility.

Another positive that came out of this situation was that I had many toxic and fake people in my life back then. This experience helped me learn who those people were. While it took me years to fight the tears because of the rumors people spread and the things people said about me, I am now stronger because of those people. I'm in a band with people I love and respect. Each step on my journey has led me to the place I am today. I am so grateful for all of it. I learned forgiveness, grace, tenacity, and have continued to pursue my dreams despite the roadblocks along the way. They were there for a reason. In Gabby Bernstein's book, *The Universe Has Your Back*, she has an entire chapter about how obstacles are detours in the right direction. When I read her book, I related so hard to this passage.

> When you choose to see your obstacles as detours in the right direction, you can begin to find a deeper meaning and personal growth amid the discomfort. Maybe you can connect to a higher purpose, make a real connection to someone, or even be set on a path that will redirect the course of your life in an ultimately positive way not otherwise

possible. All obstacles that are perceived with love can be transformed into the greatest life lessons.

When you learn who YOU are deep inside, when you come from a place of love, faith, persistence, openness, and forgiveness, you make yourself unfuckwithable. Be grateful for that adversity. Be thankful for that detour. For those are the things that make you the person you're to become. And remember, you are not your job. You are not your band. You are not what you do. You are a spiritual being, and a light sent down here to give love and spread light to everyone you come across. Learn who you are, a Spirit with a purpose, and that will put you on the path to being unfuckwithable.

Suggestions:

1. Not everything is meant to last forever. We have no control over any outcome. You can only do your best, but ultimately, what is best for you will happen, whether you want to accept that or not. Life flows much more harmoniously if you do accept it.

2. You are not your job. While you may be involved in something that you love, and that matters so much to you, if it goes away tomorrow, you will still be okay. And if it goes away tomorrow, it

was not meant to be for you; otherwise, it would always be for you. Remember, you can't lose something that's good for you.

3. If you do experience the loss of a job, the breakup of a relationship or band, or something you felt defined your life in some way, it's okay to cry that shit out. It's okay to mourn the loss of something you so dearly loved. And it's also okay to get back on those beautiful feet of yours and start over. There is no such thing as failure, but there are, as Gabrielle Bernstein shares, "detours in the right direction."

20. Trust in Your Source

No matter where you are in life, if you believe things will work out for you, THEY WILL! I PROMISE! They will work out PERFECTLY, in the perfect timing, in the perfect way. We all need to stop being little bitches about the hiccups, and do a little trusting in something bigger than we can imagine.

Like I shared earlier, I wrestled with the notion of God for the longest time in my life. I think that is maybe one of the reasons I love the band Manchester Orchestra so much. Andy Hull writes these beautiful lyrics of growing up and coming to terms with a religion he wanted to believe in, but saw so much bullshit in. In the eye opening book, *Wishes Fulfilled*, Dr. Wayne Dyer describes God, the one most of us have been raised to believe in, as a God of wrath... a jealous and angry God, one who picks and chooses who will get to do His deeds, as the God of ego.

The opening verse in the chapter entitled 'Your Highest Self' is written by Saint Paul in the New Testament of the Christian Bible in Philippians 2: 5-6. "Let this mind be in you, which was also in Christ Jesus, who, being in the form of God, did not consider it robbery to be equal with God." Dyer then goes on to say the following:

You may find it difficult at first to be able to assert to yourself that I AM GOD. But when you put it in the context of God as love (and pure love allows you to be almighty, all-knowing, and God-realized), you will, I assure you, begin to regain the omnipotence that is your essence from the moment of your transition from nonbeing (spirit) to being (human). I emphasize these teachings of Jesus to show that the declaration of I AM GOD is not only NOT in opposition to the teachings of Christianity or other spiritual practices, but is fully aligned with these earlier teachings. The reason it may seem blasphemous to say that I AM GOD is because we've adopted the God of the ego, created by humans from ego-based ideas of a God that imitates our most unholy human attributes.

It took me a long time to find someone who felt the same things I felt when it came to God and put something so bold out in the Universe. FINALLY, something was making sense. I was personally so put off by the hatred I was seeing from religious groups in the name of "God", that I stopped saying "blessed," and refused to call the Higher Force by the name "God." I only referred to God as a Higher Power or Source or as the "Universe" or the "Energy." While I've been able to conquer these deep-rooted issues over the past year, writing a book about being inspired by something bigger than me and you, and the abundance that this connection (mind and spirit) makes, has been a huge fucking step in seeing a WAYYYY bigger picture.

For years, I labeled myself agnostic because I didn't get it. I despised the religion I grew up in. I hated the God of ego, and sometimes, it still shows up. Just as recently as two days ago, I had a flashback, and started to discard a business piece of mail that had a Bible verse on it. I had to check myself before I wrecked myself. I too, am on this journey. I stopped, read the verse, which was about "afuckingbundance," which is what I'm WRITING about, and took that lesson like a champ. For too long, I've judged. It is not my place. It is my place to be accepting of ALL because we are all a part of this Universe. We are ALL God. How others find their path is up to them, and who knows, maybe their path is easier than my path? How can any of us be sure? What I do know is that I'm certainly more open and tolerant of things that I used to not be open and tolerant towards.

Now, I'm not saying we "accept" hate, intolerance, or anything of that nature, because "there's nothing we can do about it". What I am saying is, maybe we stop to pause before we get our panties into a wad, which can happen so quickly. There is so much of that negative shit in the world, but I no longer believe we can fight anger by becoming angry or conquer hate by becoming hateful. The only things we can do are love, and know that we can ALL make a difference if we are in alignment with the Source who made us because the Source is love. Well, love is my fucking religion.

We've all heard the saying, "Let go and let God." I'm finally able to fall back on that wholeheartedly because I'm seeing what love and my Source are creating in my life. Not only that, I know what it creates in the lives of others who choose to live a life based in love. Again, I know that as long as I'm in alignment with that high vibration Energy, I can honestly sit back, trust, and know I'm going to be taken care of.

That's not to say that things we perceive as negative won't happen. They absolutely will happen. It's essential to change your perception of these things to see them as learning experiences. How will we know good things if we have not experienced bad things? What is good or bad anyway? Trusting that the lessons are there for reasons we may not know yet is vital. I've said this before, and I love looking back at things I wish had worked out and finding myself thinking, "Damn, that's why that didn't happen." I get it now.

I once again encourage you to get connected and trust in your Source. Meditate, write, learn, and love. Ask your Source, "If there's anything you don't want in my life, make it so I no longer want it anymore." More trusted words from my friend, Joni: "What you have coming that is GOOD for you won't pass you by. Your job is to prepare and to trust."

Trusting in a Higher Power has been my mainstay for years, but learning that I am ALSO that Source which I trust, basically means that my rebellious attitude toward God was just my ignorance, because I AM God. And now, I'm starting to see the puzzle pieces and how they all come together. There are a million examples of this in my life. People always seem to show up in my life at the perfect moments when I am in need or have a desire. The last twelve years haven't been a cakewalk though they have held all the lessons I needed to learn during those times.

When I decided to divorce my husband of three years, which I talk about later, I had a dear friend (who was also one of my professors), and her husband take me in. They had just had a baby, and she let me stay with her for about two months. Then I needed to leave the nest, so I had this amazing opportunity to be a roommate in a kick-ass condo. The girl I was moving in with decided she wanted to move out literally the next week. So Lisa, who owned the condo, decided to keep my rent the same as if the roommate were there, and I got to live in that condo for a year before she sold it.

During this time in my life, I had started my own social media business, and was working with a company out of Indianapolis called Rainmakers. It was a company that put on events... private business coaching, round tables, and those sorts of things. My job was to help facilitate events and help meet the needs of the members by connecting them with other people. I met so many brilliant people during this part of my life. But here's more of the Universe and perfect timing shit (this is for real).

Two major female entrepreneurs in my life at the time were Hazel Walker (she was the queen bee) and Lorraine Ball. They always joked that they were frenemies. Like, friends and enemies. They were older than me, way wiser than me, and I looked up to these women and still do. Hazel is the one who gave me the idea for this book. Anyway, I needed to move out of my condo. I needed a place to live in. Hazel had this incredible house, and it was just her living there (I didn't know this at the time). So, unbeknownst to me, Lorraine and Hazel were having lunch one day, and Lorraine suggested to Hazel that she get a roommate. Sure as shit, her response to Lorraine was, "If I'm going to have a roommate, it has to be someone like Lindsay Manfredi."

At this point, I was posting on Facebook "Hey kids, looking for a roommate to move in with... Let me know if there are any leads." This isn't verbatim but you get the point. Lorraine hits me up and tells me the story. I call Hazel, and I'm moving in and living with her for the next year. She was the absolute best roommate. We both did our thing, inspired one another, and it was just perfect. And perfect timing. AND she and I BOTH won. Our Source hooked us both up. She and I are still friends as she traipses across the globe, selling her book, *Business Networking and Sex,* which she co-authored. She lives part-time in Australia and kicks ass at her BNI networking company. Not only that, she's taught me so much in my adult life. Mainly, to never live in fear. She's twice my age and went skydiving like two months ago. She's a fucking rock star and one of my rocks. As I said, she helped inspire this book. She inspires so many, and I'm honored to call her my friend.

But it's not just these two women. Anytime in my life that I've needed anything, those people have been there. One of my dear friends, Deborah Farrar, who is like a magic ray of sunshine, has always taken me in and been a friend when I've been in the "in between" spaces of my life. I used to work for her, and when we met for the first time, it was fireworks of awesome because we just got each other. She was one of the first people to introduce me to the Law of Attraction by sponsoring me in a workshop called "Beyond Your Best". This Source has ALWAYS brought into my life the right people at the right time who are now lifetime friends.

I find myself in awe and inspiration ALL of the time now. Things like this happen in my life. I'm homeless right now, room surfing, don't (didn't have) have an agent for this book yet as I'm writing it, and I'm driving a car that's twelve years old. I'm not sure where my next permanent move is, but in all this chaos is my life, I feel the most at peace of my life because I know my Source is going to pull through every time. I trust it completely. And if you do too, there is something pretty fucking awesome to be said for having peace inside your heart and soul.

Suggestions:

1. Know your power. If you don't yet, learn it. Pick up the book *Wishes Fulfilled* by Dr. Wayne Dyer. There were things this book taught me that I had been searching for my entire life, and the principles I learned from it have changed my whole outlook, and therefore, have changed my life.

2. Remember that you have no control over the outcome. Once you make your wishes known, you must give it up to the Universe. You must have absolute faith that what you truly desire and what is right for you, is already on its way.

3. Once you understand that and live your end game as if it already is, then you can relax in the faith that the perfection of your creation will come to fruition. You can be patient, you can be peaceful, and you can be love.

21. Take A Deep Breath

I'm a big believer in dream analysis. When I wake up, and my dreams are so real, I pick them apart and apply them to my life, no matter how insane or crazy it is. Well, I had a dream while I was writing this book, that I was left in a strange city that was in crumbles like it was a war-torn area. My sense in the dream was war, not a natural disaster. In the course of this dream my travel mates, who were previous band members, left the Airbnb we had rented, and even though we were to have it for one more day, the owner wouldn't let me go back inside, although I pleaded with him to let me back in. I was left alone with nowhere to go and nowhere to stay. In my dream, I felt fear. I managed to accept that I was on my own, and as I was walking away from the building, I saw this beautiful, gorgeous hotel that had JUST been newly built (this hotel was not there before I spoke with the homeowner). There were water slides and people dancing, laughing, just having a blast. I remember my thought in the dream was that this could be an opportunity for me to meet new people and inspire them. Make them feel GOOD. I even had a swimsuit in the backpack I was carrying in the dream.

It may not seem to make sense to you, but it makes all the sense in the world to me. I was going through so many changes in my life at the time of this dream. I was letting go of old relationships, patterns, and ways of thinking, and starting completely over. My takeaway from this dream is that if you're in a bad situation, or if your spirit knows you're in a bad situation, take a deep breath and then feel confident in walking away, because you need to make room for bigger and better. And always remember, everything that's created in Spirit is bigger and better because there are no limits. Remember that when you listen to that Spirit by doing what needs to be done, you are following the path of God. I know that in my dream, I took a deep breath. I've been taking a lot of those lately.

There are so many studies on consciously breathing deeply and meditation, that in my mind, I can't quite understand why everyone isn't hip to it and doing it. So yeah, we're back to this. *Time* magazine recently released a "Mindfulness Special Edition" for their magazine, which I picked up in a checkout line of a grocery store. It covered numerous types of inner work. I want to take the time to dig a little further with you, and share exactly how important breath work is when it comes to calming yourself and creating a different thought process.

According to numerous studies, breathing deeply not only has a physiological effect on your body, but it also has an emotional impact. Some of the critical findings of these studies show that meditative or deep breathing, for even just five minutes a day will boost serotonin, dopamine, and endorphins, which are all linked to creating a good mood. It has been proven to reduce pain by changing activity in key pain-processing regions of the brain. In one study, those who meditated experienced a 40% reduction in pain intensity. It can also reduce stress-induced inflammation from conditions such as arthritis and asthma. Meditative breathing also helps relax the body to the point that digestion runs more smoothly. It has also been shown to lower blood pressure, and in one study, those who meditated for 20 minutes, twice a day lowered their blood pressure by 5 mm Hg. (Not sure what that means, as I'm not a biology girl, but I'm guessing it's a big deal.)

I know I keep saying this, but life has all kinds of unexpected twists, turns, and bumps that are going to happen. How we react to them has either positive or negative long-term effects on our mental health, which in turn manifests itself in our physical health. Now, I am no doctor, I am only one who immerses myself in education on these things, so I'm sharing what I've learned. There are a plethora of studies from which you can get exact details about what I've shared. This is also not intended as medical advice and anyone experiencing health issues should contact their medical provider.

In my personal life, I've found that by taking a deep breath, it allows me to come back to the present moment, and gives me a chance to shift my thoughts. I'm able to be an outside observer of my thoughts, which in turn allows me to shift to a different headspace consciously.

Do you want to feel bad? Or do you want to feel good? Breathing allows me the room to have complete control over my emotions and how I want to react to a situation. It's pretty fucking crazy the difference I feel, and the shifts of perspective that taking a deep breath has caused in my life. I honestly no longer give a shit what other people think, feel, or say about me, but it doesn't always start that way. I may have an initial knee-jerk reaction to something or may get offended or hurt. But, the more I "practice" breathing, and being centered in Spirit and disconnected from this feeling of angst or a situation that is fleeting, the more I am fully aware that I have this pact with God: Please make it so that I no longer want anything that is bad in my life.

Once you process things in this manner, it's easy to let go of the shit that you've been holding onto, for the sake of growing and evolving into a better human being. You can then shift that energy into something positive and tell everyone else to go fuck themselves, in the nicest way possible.

I urge you, when you are feeling overwhelmed, stressed out, or in panic mode, to take a few moments, find a quiet space, and just breathe. It can help put things into perspective. There is no sense in worrying about the things you can't change. What you CAN change are your reactions and your thoughts. Here is another list of things you can change and control from an Instagram account I follow called "thinkgrowprosper." I have a screenshot of this on my phone so I can be reminded of what's what.

Things you can control:

1. Your beliefs
2. Your attitude
3. Your thoughts
4. Your perspective
5. How honest you are
6. Who your friends are
7. What books you read
8. How often you exercise
9. The type of food you eat
10. How many risks you take
11. How you interpret situations
12. How kind you are to others
13. How kind you are to yourself
14. How often you say "I love you"
15. How often you say "thank you"
16. How you express your feelings
17. Whether or not you ask for help

18. How often you practice gratitude

19. How many times you smile today

20. The amount of effort you put forth

21. How you spend/invest your money

22. How much time you spend worrying

23. How often you think about your past

24. Whether or not you judge other people

25. Whether or not you try again after a setback

26. How much you appreciate the things you have

If you look at it, that's a pretty intense list of things that it would serve you better to be thinking about. Who do YOU want to be tomorrow, and how can you start that today, at THIS moment? What do you want to manifest in your life, and how can you begin that change inside by changing the way you think about things?

Life is a series of moments. So, live in them, then let them go so you can free yourself for the next one to be even better. This practice begins with one deep breath and the acknowledgment that life is bigger than you.

Suggestions:

1. Take some time to spend with yourself so you can get connected

to your Spirit and the all-providing Source that is continually providing everything you need in every moment in time. Even if it's just five minutes, give yourself some space to breathe.

2. If there is a situation you encounter today that gives you any sort of anxiety, step outside of that for a moment. Just be an observer of the feeling rather than being taken away by it. Notice how it feels in your body. Notice the sensations you have and the thoughts that follow. Now that you accept the feelings, turn them around to a loving thought that serves your true nature, which comes from a place of love.

3. For the next week, commit to five minutes of quiet time a day and notice how your body, mind, and soul feel after these five minutes. Are you more peaceful? Did you have any creative ideas come to you? Were you able to handle a situation in a better manner than you would have before? How do you FEEL? Jot these things down in a journal. Perhaps these first five minutes will turn into something much bigger for you in your life. Remember, this book came to me while I was in a meditation practice. I decided to act upon that inspiration despite never having written a book in my life.

22. Let Go of the Shit (Especially Shit Food)

Last night, I had another dream. Please keep in mind that as I write this book, I, too, am an inspired Spirit in this human experience, learning every day. I just went through the breakup of a relationship I was in for about three years.

I'm also currently reading Dr. Wayne Dyer's book, *Living An Inspired Life*, which is life-altering. So, in this dream I had last night, I was in a home where I was staying on the first level and someone else lived on the second level. Someone was with me, I'm not sure who it was or who it represented in my dream, but I smelled smoke. I then looked up and saw that there was a fire raging out of control in a window of the second floor. I remember screaming, "We have to get out NOW!" So, I grabbed my computer bag and my guitar, and with my girlfriend at my heels, ran out and set them on the ground. I was convinced I could get one more trip in to grab some "important" stuff, and just as I was on my way to get more of my things, the second floor caved in on the first. There was no longer anything left. It was all going up in flames before my eyes.

I believe my dream was a direct in-Spirit message to me this morning. Let go of the stuff. Let go of the shit that no longer serves you. Those things I saved in my dream were my computer to write, and my bass to play. Those two things are the only two things I need in my real life right now.

You see, sometimes, we have to take a step fucking back and recognize that starting over can be the most freeing thing ever. Recognize what's in your life and what's holding you back, mentally and emotionally. Just as Dyer says in *Living an Inspired Life*, "Unclutter your life." His advice – "If you haven't worn it in the past year or two, recycle it for others to use. – Get rid of old files that take up space and are seldom, if ever needed – Donate unused toys, tools, books, bicycles, and dishes to a charitable organization."

If you take the time to do this (I am going through this process also), I promise, something inside shifts and weight is lifted off your shoulders.

I have a good friend named Amber. She lived in Indianapolis when I was living there. She is such a beautiful soul that words can't begin to describe her. She worked at Riley Children's Hospital in the cancer ward and spent her days playing with the children who were going through some of the worst days of their lives. She gave love, playtime, and hope to these precious children. But after years and years of doing this, she knew she needed a shift because, while she loved her work, it was beginning to take a toll on her. She never really thought about herself and what she loved to do or needed to do to make her heart sing.

So, one day, she just called me up and said, "I'm selling

everything I own and buying a one-way ticket to St. Croix. I have to get out of Indianapolis." She didn't know what she was going to do when she got there, but she needed to follow her gut and make a change in her life, because she just wasn't happy.

It's been four years since her move, and I've never seen such a dramatic shift in someone. She is now on a team that charters a gorgeous boat all over the Caribbean. They make the most magnificent food for their guests, and she is in the relationship of her dreams. Her physical body also changed because she's happy. She is healthy and makes different decisions based on feeling good. She changed her entire life for the better because she decided to follow her Spirit, and despite not knowing what was to come, she had faith in her Source, and that Source has never failed to provide for her. She's one of the most inspiring people I know.

Now, as you're letting go of stuff and making room for what you genuinely need, maybe it's a good time to analyze the foods that you've been feeding your body. Do you eat until you're satisfied or do you eat until you're so stuffed you can barely move? What's in the kitchen that's holding you back? Is your refrigerator full of live foods, or is it full of unhealthy processed foods? Do you eat out of legitimate hunger or out of boredom or the need for fulfillment? These are questions to ask yourself if you're not where you want to be physically. While you're clearing out the clutter in your life and your home, perhaps now is the time to throw out those cookies or chips or any other junk food that makes you feel like junk. They call it that for a reason.

Your body is nourished with "life" food, and everyone has a different chemical makeup. If you'd like to learn more about finding out what works for YOUR body, I urge you to pick up one of Lyn-Genet Recitas New York Times Bestsellers, *The Plan* or *The Metabolism Plan*. Her research on nutrition and inflammation caused by the foods we eat has changed lives across the globe. It has caused people to go off of medication and lose thousands of pounds of weight, by giving individuals proper nutrients and exercises to perform at an optimum level. I live my life through her research, and her *Plan Cookbook* is AMAZING! I know how I feel when I'm in the groove and eating well. There is a direct reflection of it in everything in my life, from how I work out to how my brain performs creatively. I feel it in my clothes and I feel it in my bones. Feed your body. Feed it well. But ultimately, get rid of the excess junk in all areas of life to make room for the bigger, better, and brighter, that's currently on its way.

Suggestions:

1. Today, I encourage you to clear out the clutter. Go through your

car, your filing cabinets, your closet, and your cupboards. I would encourage you to get rid of anything you haven't used in over two years. This can have a profound effect on how you feel. There's truly something to be said for a little bit of organization, even if it's a little bit of organization in the little bit of chaos.

2. I would encourage you to ask yourself today, as you're doing this, how you can serve others with some of the things you're getting rid of.

3. You can fucking do this.

23. Your Pet Peeves Don't Fucking Matter – It's Just Your Ego

While we're on the path of getting rid of things you don't need in your life, here's another thing you may want to consider examining…your pet peeves. I was married from 2006-2009. During this time, I had a teenage stepdaughter. She was 13-16 during the marriage, and my daughter was three to six years old. Now, I don't know what my fucking problem was. For some reason, which I can't explain, I just had some significant issues with the way I thought my ex-husband was parenting. To me, he was his daughter's friend and pretty much let her do whatever she wanted and dress however she wanted. I was never okay with this. This situation led to A LOT of resentment, anger, frustration, and a lot of unrest in me, which ultimately led to our divorce. Looking back now, I wish I would've just RELAXED a little and not been such a control freak. Would that have made a difference in our marriage? I don't know. Perhaps. Perhaps not.

I'm a little embarrassed to admit this, but I mean, I'd get fucking PISSED if her computer cord was plugged in and her computer was not attached to the end of it. Like it was going to make the electricity bill go up or something. It was ridiculous. In that sense, I was acting just like my parents and just wanting to be authoritarian. Whatever, it doesn't matter now; I was a fucking bitch. And I can see this now.

Had I been more in tune with HER rather than her fucking computer cord, everyone involved would have been better off. I mean, the stress I put on myself because I wanted to be in control, I see now it was a wicked display of my ego at work. I had NO right to judge her.

Teenage years are tough enough with school and friends and trying to figure out if and when it's all going to make sense. I should've relaxed. I recently found out that she was in a terrible accident. She was hit by a car and is going through serious therapy to restore her body and her mind. The interesting thing was that she had just moved to begin her Doctoral degree. She was a Clinical and Cognitive Neuroscience Researcher and Doctoral Student at a major university. I'm not sure what is going to happen, but I follow her progress, I pray for her healing, and I believe that God has a plan. I think he put her in this situation to understand and experience in the brain everything she has been researching. I believe she is going to make considerable changes in the study when she can. It has been a long road for her so far, that I can't even begin to comprehend. I believe she is a miracle in progress.

While I can't take back the past, I do see the mistakes I made, and look at them as blessings on the road to becoming who I am today. It makes me look at the things that make me tick. It's made me change the way I see things that others do and realize I just have to shut up because I'm not in their shoes. And I also love it when I'm talking and say something like, "My biggest pet peeve is when someone interrupts me," and then ten minutes later, I find myself interrupting someone.

What I'm asking you to consider is letting go of the judgments we so often catch ourselves in. That isn't to say you or I won't have them, but it is asking you to be aware of them so you can immediately stop that way of thinking and turn it into something positive, thereby raising a low energy to a high, vibrant one. It can happen within seconds, and it's a beautiful thing to witness when it occurs. You see your growth, which in turn gives you even more to be grateful about.

Changing your language and how you see things is so crucial to your success as a human being. It makes the difference in getting to a place of abundance from a place of lack. It's coming from fear to love. It's coming from judgment to acceptance. It's accepting everyone and everything for who they are and what it is in that moment in time, and being entirely at peace with it. Think about it, can you change the way things are or the way other people see things? No. But you CAN change the way you view, perceive, and accept things in your feelings.

There's something I'd like to share with you from Dr.

Wayne Dyer's *Change Your Thoughts, Change Your Life*. It speaks to the point of looking inward and how our ego gets in the way of allowing, which then causes resistance and frustration when things aren't going the way we "think" they "should be" going. I'm sharing this because we so quickly want to control how people are being when we're looking outward. One thing he says is "Discontinue deciding what anyone else should or shouldn't be doing." He then goes on to say:

> Avoid thoughts and activities that involve telling people who are perfectly capable of making their own choices what to do. In your family, remember that you do not own anyone.
>
> This is always true. In fact, disregard any inclination to dominate in ALL of your relationships. Listen, rather than expound. Pay attention to yourself when you're having judgmental opinions and see where self-attention takes you. When you replace an ownership mentality with one of allowing, you'll begin to see the true unfolding of the Tao (The Way) in yourself and other people. From that moment on, you'll be free of frustration with those who don't behave according to your ego-dominated expectations.

I guess the main point it comes down to is, would you rather feel irritated and annoyed by someone else's behavior? Or would you rather have a peace inside you that no one can affect? Would you rather feel bad? Or would you rather feel good? Would you rather live in a low vibrating energy environment? Or would you rather live in a high vibrating energy environment?

There are times when I am not operating at my best levels. As soon as I even think, "I am the highest vibration of love in the Universe," I have an immediate vibration shift in my body. If I'm beginning to get a sore throat, if I immediately switch my thoughts from, "I am getting sick," to, "I am in perfect health. Thank you for a body that heals itself," there is an immediate difference in the way I feel.

As I said, this isn't about not having the shitty thoughts. It's about learning how to shift them immediately. And once you begin to consciously change your thoughts, then it will eventually become an unconscious shift, and you'll be living in a flow where things are just as they are, and you no longer have any pet peeves because they simply do not matter nor do you need that negative energy in your life. It's a real feeling in your body and your soul when you allow yourself to tune into it.

Suggestions:

1. If you are a stepparent or a parent in general, I know it is not always easy. I urge you today to let go of your ego's need to control everything, and instead live from a place of love. Try sitting down with your child and having a real conversation with him or her about your feelings. Also let the conversation go both ways. Your actions may be a cause of resentment for the other party. I encourage you just to be open because openness and acceptance allow room for relationships to flourish.

2. If you feel you've already let your pet peeves and unconscious behavior get the best of you in the past, it's okay. If you think that you've already "screwed" something up, I'd like to remind you again, that you can't lose something that's good for you, even if you lost it because of your behavior. If something or someone is no longer in your life, then it was a lesson you needed to learn. And the same lessons will continue to show up until you get it. But regardless, please forgive yourself. Please be gentle with yourself. Please love yourself because you can't expect any of these things from others until you first have them in you.

3. By now, I hope you're seriously considering the role your ego has had in making things not so great in your life. I hope you're beginning to see the difference between ego, and self-love and love

for others. If someone is doing something that bothers you, for example chewing with his or her mouth open, or grinding their teeth, have a kind, loving conversation with them about how it makes you feel. But in everything you do, please do it with love. And as most kids need reminding over and over and over again until it sticks, remember, you probably needed reminders as well when you were that age.

24. *When We Look Inward – Not Outward*

In a world full of social media and endless distractions, I find it amusing and disturbing that we tend to look everywhere for answers other than inward. We'd discover answers are most readily available to us by looking inward when we are in the midst of something serious. I've been super guilty of this. It's so much easier to distract yourself than to get real with yourself. It's so much easier to look out rather than in. It's easier to place blame than take responsibility for our decisions amidst the chaos. There have been countless times, as I've been going through considerable changes in my life, where I've not been disciplined enough to get real with myself. Or, I should say, I DO get real with myself, but I procrastinate like a high school kid with ADHD, writing a term paper.

The last separation I went through was not easy at all. This person had been a normal part of my life for over four years. Even though we had only been together as a couple for a little over half that time, it was still tricky. Our relationship had cancer in it, and I had to walk away to regain my identity because it got lost. I was unhappy, I was angry, and I was not myself for a while there, way longer than I like to admit. It's like my spirit was steadily getting buried in all the expectations someone else had of me. There was so much hypocrisy in the entire thing. I just couldn't take it. And I couldn't take getting yelled at all the time. It's crazy how I allowed things to get so out of control. But me walking away was necessary to get back in alliance with my Source and forgive myself for the shit that I went through as a result of staying out of habit and security.

In the book *Co-Creating at Its Best – A Conversation Between Two Masters,* Dr. Wayne Dyer and Esther Hicks are in a deep conversation with Abraham, the Collective Consciousness. Dr. Dyer is discussing dysfunctional relationships, and Abraham responds with, "…if you were more unwilling to put up with negative emotions, your lives would go a whole lot better for you. You have trained yourselves to be willing to endure misalignment."

Think about that for a moment. We have TRAINED ourselves to be willing to endure misalignment. In other words, we have trained ourselves to stop listening to our inner voice. And in this time and place we're in, full of social media and endless "hook up" apps, it's easy to just dive into something (or someone) else to feed an ego that wants to be fed. Or we may distract ourselves with a show or a movie and SOMETHING that makes us not have to look at US for just a while longer. I do it all the time, but I've been making a conscious effort NOT to do it as much.

There are a million people I could call to hang out with, a million tweets I could distract myself with, a million Facebooks and Instagram posts to stare at to avoid the uneasy feeling of being on my own again. And I'm not gunna lie, I have distracted myself with all of these things and plenty of times to top it off. But that's not what HELPS me get to where I'm going. I've had to make a conscious effort to put my phone down, not to text people because I'm bored or feeling alone, and to make decisions based on taking time for me. And no, I've not been perfect at any of this. However, I HAVE been aware of when it's happening, which is step number one for me.

The interesting thing is, with all of this social media trolling, I'm so much more determined to get this book done. I feel there are so many people so lost in the drama of their own lives when it could be so much easier. Let's make life easier. Doesn't that seem way better than making it harder on ourselves?

Even "friendly advice" from friends can be a distraction from looking inward. I have some fantastic friends these days. It's funny because I've had them for a while, and my true girlfriends are older and wiser than me. They have ALWAYS been there, in every facet of my adult life. I am blessed to have them. However, I don't want them to have to listen to my drama all the time. So, these days, I'm pretty private about whom I share things with, because they don't need to hear that my ex got drunk again and lost his shit on me, just like the last time. It's fucking embarrassing. And deep down, I know what I need to do on a daily basis. However, I'm incredibly thankful to have a support system of women who have my back, and were willing to listen to the same story over and over again. But I don't want to do that anymore. The point is, when you hear yourself telling that same story over and over again. It's insanity. And I hope you can find the balls, like I had to, to get out of a bad situation in which you're not truly able to be who you are here to be. Selfish love is no good. And when you genuinely look inside, in your heart of hearts, you have a vibrating feeling. It's good or bad. Always go with your gut. UNTRAIN your misaligned mind.

For me, a quiet space helps me to focus on me. That may be why I love my meditation practice so much. It has genuinely transformed my spiritual being, and changed my life in the process. I'm not sure this book would have been born had I not been in that space at that moment. Or it would have, but perhaps it would have been years to come. But, because I was able to look inside, this happened out of that, which occurred out of Spirit. Again, perfect orchestration.

I'm going to wrap this up because I think you get the point. When you're going through something serious, or if you need change in your life, make it a priority. Listen to your heart. Listen to your soul. Fuck what your head has to say because logic is sometimes a happiness stealer. I've experienced that in past relationships and won't ever live there again. I don't want you to live there either. Live in a magical place where the seemingly impossible happens. Be a unicorn and shit. That's what happens when you look inward, not outward.

Suggestions:

1. I'm not going to try to tell you what to do, but I will say this. Airing your dirty laundry on any form of social media doesn't reflect too well on the person doing it. While it may feel like you're getting attention and you want to feel like people are on your "side," it doesn't make your situation any better. May I encourage you to stop and think about what you're doing the next time you are tempted to do it. Ask yourself if your words are building people up or tearing them down? Ask yourself what it is you truly need. And perhaps some alone time will help.

2. I recently read that if you think about something for seventeen seconds, it will produce more and more of the same thoughts and in turn, you'll be vibrating at that frequency. The Law of Attraction will hold onto this and give you more of the same because that is where your antenna is tuned into. Change your old ways of thinking back to where you originated. You are from Source Energy that is nothing but love and abundance. When you tap into that energy, you will have the entire world open up to you. Keep your thoughts on the

blessings. Keep your heart focused inward and upward at the same time. Listen to your body. Listen to your soul.

3. All of the answers you need for the tough decisions you need to make are right there inside of you. When you're changing your life for the better, you will always have support along the way, even if you don't see it right away. This has happened to me so many times. The wonderful Dr. Wayne Dyer always says, "When you believe it, you'll see it." Take these fine words of wisdom and apply them to any situation you're in.

25. *Take A Social Media Break – And Don't Fucking Announce It*

Seriously. Put down your phone, your computer, your tablet, whatever your drug of choice is. We don't have to know you're going to be off the grid for a day, or however long you decide to get unplugged. I've owned a social media marketing company for going on ten years now. I understand. I get caught up in the bullshit too, hence why you're reading this. It's incredible to me how much time I waste scrolling through Facebook, Twitter, Instagram, or any other number of things that distract me. Can I have all that time back please, to be working on something productive and of value? Nope.

I recently had a conversation with a good friend, who also happens to be an incredible singer. He had close to 10K Instagram followers at one time, and he told me he spent hours upon hours thinking about another selfie of him that would make him look "hot." People would always "like" his photos and comment on them, and if a particular picture didn't get as many "likes" or comments, he would delete it, and that shit would affect his mood, and then affect his entire day. Also, he told me he would later spend even more time thinking about the next photo to get more likes and comments to feed his ego. This is how addictive and compelling social media can be if you let it take over how you see yourself. The beautiful thing is that one night he realized this destructive, egocentric behavior and just deleted his account. He said it made him sick to his stomach to see all of these photos of just HIM.

It's amazing to me and my buddy that we live in such a narcissistic culture of always needing attention from people we don't even fucking know. It's high time we get the fuck off for a little bit, and pay attention to the people actually IN our lives...our friends, family, CHILDREN (if you have them). I mean, that's what's important. When we're lying on our deathbed, I highly doubt any of us will look back and think, "Damn, if I only could've checked my Facebook one more time." No, we'd most likely instead be thinking, "If only I would've spent more time OFF my phone/computer and been IN the moment with the people I gave a shit about."

Social media has a time and a place, but social media, the number of followers you have, or how many "likes" you have don't FUCKING define WHO you are as a person. YOU define who you are as a person. And when I see someone who take selfies every day and posts them, I see someone who needs A LOT of attention, which makes me wonder why that is. Yeah, you're cute. Get over yourself and do something to make the world a better place. Go fuck yourselfie. Again, I've been guilty of ALL of this. That's why I'm okay saying it. I mean, I take selfies every once in a while, when I'm having a good hair or makeup day, or whatever, but these aren't every day, and I certainly don't get enough likes or comments to feed my ego. I'm not that popular. I can see that desire to be wanted, and it can indeed be a slippery slope.

Maybe taking some time off will help you see how much time you're wasting on these platforms. Perhaps you'll be able to sit back and see what makes you tick, or what makes you want the attention. Maybe you'll be able to get to the root of what it is you truly desire. It's okay to establish specific times when you spend a few minutes catching up and seeing what events are coming up, see what your friends are up to, or posting/sharing cool shit. That's fine. And a selfie every once in a while, is fine too! I'm just encouraging you to get out there and EXPERIENCE life. Make it bigger and better for you, and make the world a better place by engaging in what's actually in front of your face, not your computer. You're gorgeous, and the world needs to see you.

Suggestions:

1. Unplug.
2. Remember that you are perfect and amazing, and you don't need anyone else to tell you that. Love yourself. Love yourself as hard as you can.
3. Get out in the world and share your beauty.

26. Take A YOU Day – A WHOLE Fucking Day

When is the last time you took some time to do what YOU wanted to do? When is the last time you had a pedicure, a massage, or hell, even a nap? When is the last time you lost track of time because you were in such a state of joy and bliss, and what was it that you were doing to cause those 'lose track of time' moments?

Whether you're single or married, have children or no children, sometimes one of the most important things you can do on your way to inspired badassery is to take time for YOURSELF. And I'm not just talking to the women here. I'm talking to the men as well.

I'm just going to tell you about my day today because it was one that I needed. It's only after the New Year as I'm writing this particular section. I'm heading to Phoenix in two days to get back into the studio. I have so much to do. I'm working on this book, I'm working on my social media job with a comedy club, and I have to nail out this book proposal that is taking me way too long to do, according to my schedule. Also, I've been getting myself back on the "work until 3 am schedule" that rock and roll often requires. (Btw, I am not complaining about ANY of this). I get to live my dreams and get to do so with an incredible support system. But today was one of those days where it didn't matter how many cups of coffee I drank, it didn't matter what fun stuff was going on in LA, it didn't matter that it was my last couple of days here to spend with those I care about. I couldn't handle anything about the world.

I woke up and meditated. I read an ass-ton of Dr. Wayne Dyer along with another book I'm reading on quantum physics. Then I took my ass back to bed and slept most of the day. I needed it. I needed to listen to my body. As I was laying there doing my best not to beat myself up by saying things like, "You should work out...you should write one chapter... you need to shower because it's been like, days..." I finally had to shut my mind up, and thank the Universe for allowing me the understanding that sometimes, I need to rest. And today was a rest day, as tough as it may have been to my ego-dominating mind that needs to achieve more.

At 5 pm, after lying around all day, I got up to wash the dishes. That gave me a little motivation to get some workout clothes on. Then a little motivation to do at least a 30-minute Insanity workout with permission to do my best and not worry about "killing it." I just needed to move. You've heard that saying, "There's never been a workout I've regretted" (unless it's Crossfit). But you get the point. I didn't regret it at all and ended up giving it my all. There was no way I could have done that without the rest I had during the day.

The Four Agreements was one of the first audiobooks on

self-improvement I ever listened to. It was the first book that introduced me to this world of self-exploration that I'm currently in, so you could say it changed the course of my life. Well, I tend to beat myself up often, and have been on a quest to exchange the beatings for more uplifting conversations with myself. One of the agreements I am so fond of is the one that says to always do your best, and some days your best is better than others. Well, I know some days I have mad productive days. Today, in my day of nothingness, it was as productive in its own right. I was able to rest.

Perhaps it was the rest I was able to get for that half of a day that will keep me from getting the flu for a week. My body and my Spirit know that I'm about to embark on a crazy busy month. I had to listen to that, even if it meant feeling completely lazy all day. In the midst of all of this, I've gotten many things done that I had on my list. I was at my best at the times I did them.

Maybe you don't need an entire day to nap. Perhaps you need to get out in nature. Or maybe you need some time with a close friend who helps you stay grounded and balanced. Whatever you need, listen to your heart. Listen to your body. Listen to your Spirit and then honor what you hear.

Today, I am so grateful to have taken a "me" day. I highly suggest you do the same when you need it.

Suggestions:

1. When it comes to taking care of your needs first, this is not selfish. Self-love and care are necessary. Let me repeat the line from the Introduction: You are the MOST important person in your life. You can't help anyone to your fullest potential if you're not getting the proper rest, care, etc., that you need. If anyone wants to make you feel bad about it, fuck 'em! Yes, that person is an asshole.

2. It's okay not to want to do something or not to have the energy to do something. In a world where it's go-go-go, achieve-achieve-achieve, do-do-do, we must break out of that ego drive and just rest. There's a time for rest. The Universe created you to enjoy all of the things, so, enjoy that shit.

3. Always, ALWAYS, listen to your heart and always, ALWAYS love yourself. You are beautiful in every way. Believe that.

27. Listen to Your Favorite Album on Full Blast

While you're taking a "you" day, get down with the music. Play a little. Act like the free spirit you are. Get in connection with your true nature. I'm the biggest dork when it comes to acting like a kid. I swear, if I'm around people, I'll go into the restroom and do the silliest, funniest, "get down" dance I can, to reunite myself with play. And I can't even begin to talk about the power of music, and how it saved my life during the times I needed saving. Hell, it saved me even when I didn't need saving. And as much as silence is good for the soul, so is music. Sometimes, you have to let go and be in the moment with your favorite songs. Don't be afraid to lock your doors, pull your shades, and get all *Risky Business* wherever you are. You could probably use it.

When I was a kid, I couldn't wait to get the house to myself, so I could play music as loud and pretend it was me up there on stage. I didn't just act, I FELT it. As an adult, I can now see that my vibration led me to get to live my dreams. And in this alone time, I learned so much about music by just listening to it. I would dissect the songs, listening first to the lyrics, guitars, bass, drums, and then dissecting the song structure and the hooks. It was everything to me then, and it still is now. I get so down with it, that when I'm working or going to sleep, I can't have anything other than meditation music playing because I will get sucked right into a song and hear ALL of it. My daughter is the same way. She tells me she can't wait for everyone to leave the house so she can sing at the top of her lungs. She thrives in her alone music time, and I respect the shit out of that.

Hell, I'll take a good road trip if I need to get some music time in. Being in the music industry, being able to talk to so many amazing artists and hear the backstories of their journeys and the impact music made on their lives is one of my favorite things to hear. I used to sit for hours and watch *Behind The Music* on VH1 back in the day. I'm amazed at how some songs can take me back to distinct times in my life, feelings I had during those times, and even smells that can arise because of the power music has.

In 2016, CNN covered a study done in Australia from the Australian Unity Wellbeing Index. This study is an annual survey that attempts to measure the happiness of Australian citizens. In 2014, the Index focused on music consumption habits through six different activities, which included listening to music, singing, playing an instrument, dancing, composing music, and attending music-oriented events.

According to CNN, Deakin University's Melissa Weinberg, who co-authored the study, told CNN there were specific activities that seemed to correlate with higher happiness levels. She said, "We found there were differences in those who danced or attended music events." She also told them that active engagement was critical because "people who intentionally interact with music, they're using an outlet to express their emotions."

"Music seems to be a way that can facilitate social connections," Weinberg says. "And we know social relationships are critical to subjective wellbeing. Anything that has people coming together through mutual interest or commonality will contribute to this, including music."

SO, not only is music something in my life that keeps me happy and is good for my soul, it's good for EVERYONE'S soul. As I said earlier, I don't have music on 24/7 because I also respect the quiet time I have, but man, don't be afraid to get down. And if you play music, kudos to you. Keep it up, and never compromise on what you create. If it comes from you and your Spirit, then it's perfect.

The CNN report I referenced can be found here: (http://www.cnn.com/2016/08/17/health/music-concerts-dancing-study-trnd/)

Suggestions:

1. Close your blinds.

2. Turn it up.

3. Tune everything else out.

28. Shut the Fuck Up Sometimes

There. I said it. Shut the fuck up. Really.

When is the last time you didn't express your opinion and felt 1000% okay with it? When you can get THERE, that's saying something about your character. Too often, we speak because we can. We have a million platforms to be heard from which, most of the time, are our ignorant opinions. We tend to have a response to people without actually listening and hearing what they say. So many people argue to argue, to be "right." I promise it can be truly taxing on your soul if you want to be "right" all the time.

While being open and honest is a good thing in certain situations, there are times when other people can suck the life out of us, and like the victim, the ego would like to think we are, we HAVE TO react. What people say, think, do, feel, and how they respond to their environments and circumstance is their karma. How we react to them or our situation and circumstance is ours.

When we can be in a state of being, always knowing that the Universe is there for US, little needs to be said, and there's something to be said for a bit of detachment.

I was having a discussion with my bandmate, Nick Coyle, about this very thing. We recently had a bunch of people in a big uproar over the whole NFL kneeling thing, and we were just amazed by all the people who just fell right in with the "my opinion somehow needs to be heard and matters." No, it doesn't, and no, it doesn't. I sometimes wonder at what point are people going to get tired of bickering over some bullshit someone says on the Internet, where half the time, they're arguing over nothing. STOP. PLEASE STOP FEEDING THE MACHINE OF SEPARATION AND DISCONTENTMENT.

We cannot change or control people. We are here to be lovers. As Dr. Dyer always said, we are spiritual beings here having a human experience. We WANTED to be here. We CHOSE to be here, and we used to be full of this love and light and excitement. Then we started letting the opinions of others dim our fucking light, and we started doubting our hearts, and on and on down the deep dark path of where "just be normal" begins. Meh.

I've always been a person who needs a project. I've always been someone who wants to take people under my wing and "show them the way." Not anymore. Every individual is on his or her path and must experience whatever they must to get where they need to be. And no matter what path that person chooses, we all go back to our Source. We return to that where we came from when this experience ends as a human. All we can do is love, with no exception. Forgive with no need to have it returned. Give with no expectation.

I don't feel like I need to change people anymore. I honestly look to see myself in everyone I make eye contact with. What I do see is that, if someone is not vibrating on the same level as me, that's okay. I don't think I'm better than anyone, but I will choose to stay in alignment with those of the same energy as me so I can continue to expand my mind, heart, and soul. It takes you back to that self-love and self-care again. No one could tell me what to do when I wasn't ready to hear it. But boy, when you're ready to make a change, you're ready, and nothing can stop change.

I've been reading the Tao Te Ching over the last month, and the 56th verse of this 2500-year-old manuscript addresses this with the line, "Close your mouth." Too often, we speak without thinking about what's coming out of our mouths. Or we talk to try to win the approval of others. A passage in Dr. Dyer's *Change Your Thoughts, Change Your Life* addresses this along with getting honest with yourself:

> Get honest with yourself about wanting to win the favor of others. You don't have to prove anything to anyone, and you'll never succeed by droning on and on. Remember that "those who talk do not know" or as one translation of this verse simply states, "Shut your mouth." Silence is your evidence of inner knowing. Talking to convince others

actually says more about your need to be right than their need to hear what you have to say! So rather than trying to persuade others, keep quiet…just enjoy that deeply satisfying inner awareness.

Change comes from within people. Your opinion or voice, or anger only adds fuel to a ridiculous fire. Most of the time, especially in this politically charged environment we're currently in, your opinion is NOT going to change the minds of others. Let people be people. Let them have their opinions. Listen to them, be compassionate, and it's OKAY not to agree. It's far more encouraging for others to see you listening and respecting an opinion or thought pattern different from your own. So, sometimes, nothing needs to be said. I promise, silence speaks far louder than words. Stop giving in to stupid Facebook or Twitter posts that don't go with the way you think or want them to go. Just say "fuck it" and go, do YOU. Be the best YOU can be. True peace and change can lie in doing just that.

Suggestions:

1. Notice your thoughts and feelings today when someone says or does something you don't agree with. Notice how it makes you feel, and maybe not retaliate with your opinion or more words to divide.

Instead focus on uniting, and that unity may just happen by keeping your mouth shut.

2. Get off the Internet and go live your life. If there is something you feel needs to be changed, go BE the change. But don't fight for it. Remember that things come easy when you're in true alignment with Source, and are focused on love rather than revenge or fighting. We can't fight our way to peace. It's not of Spirit. We can love our way to peace, though. There is a massive difference between the two paths. One is of least resistance and operates on a much higher vibration.

3. If you are not in alignment with people, walk away. Go back to #2. Actions speak much louder than words. Be love. Be the change. Don't be a part of the madness.

29. Practice Compassion

I feel like shutting the fuck up is a good segue into compassion. What I just wrote in the previous chapter about trying to convince others 'that they're wrong and I'm right' is something I still work on, especially with my family. But I'm getting there. I mean, how easy is it to get on a high horse when we're experiencing some enlightenment or "a-ha" moment. Then how easy is it to judge others when they don't see things our way? Fucking easy, I know, you know. It's a matter of understanding when to keep our mouths shut and simply saying, "Thank you for explaining your point of view. I may not have considered that before," can change a relationship in a heartbeat. It is growth when we feel our blood boiling, and we start wanting to say something, or argue to prove our "point" but then choose not to. It makes me think of the old saying, "You catch more flies with honey…"

In my world, I've never seen eye to eye with either of my siblings in terms of religion, God, all that stuff. I believe the Universe is God, and God is in everything in the Universe, including ourselves. Therefore, we are all God, and have the power to manifest anything we want when we tap into our Source through prayer and meditation. So far in my life, I've really never been happier, healthier, more centered, or professionally satisfied. So this works for me. I live a life of abundance. I think everyone should live this way, because there's plenty of abundance to go around, and there's plenty of Source that keeps expanding.

On the other hand, I grew up in a home that didn't teach abundance. We always had everything we needed and lived a nice middle-class life. However, we learned to hold tight to money, watch what you spend, and continually heard the phrases, "we can't afford that" or "we need a coupon." We couldn't do this, or we couldn't do that because there was never enough. I was also taught that God was an angry and jealous God, but would randomly show grace to those who admitted their sins and turned away from them. Oh, and the only way you could get to "heaven" was through Jesus. Whoa. Too much for me. I was forced to march to the beat of my own drum, which was, "I can do anything, and I can have anything I want." It has paid off, but I had to reprogram with meditation.

I've been working on my relationship with both of my parents. I've been sharing things, books and meditations especially, that have had a direct impact on my state of mind and being, hoping they will take some tidbits of wisdom and apply it to their lives. (Talk about some weird role reversal.) I want to see all of my family, and everyone for that matter, living in abundance, not worrying about anything because the Universe is in control and will always work things out, which makes it easy to give, to let go, and not be so uptight. However, I was severely tested in the compassion department when I asked my Mom if I could borrow her car while she was out of town for the weekend on my recent visit back home. I was headed to Michigan to see one of my favorite bands, Highly Suspect, which was playing about five hours from where I was staying.

I didn't have my car, which was in California, but my dad had a truck he was letting me use. The main reason I wanted to take her car was because of the shitty gas mileage my dad's truck got. Well, she said no for all these reasons, wondering what could happen. Then, in the end, she was like, "No, it's my car, and I don't want anyone using it." This pissed me off. I'm using this as a lesson I had to learn to be more compassionate.

I was so upset because, in my opinion, she didn't care about helping me, and of course I was making it about me. She was going out of town and wasn't using her car because her friend was driving. She was only thinking about her precious vehicle; that means nothing. Also, in my mind, I had been living with a very giving family. Anytime my boyfriend (at the time) or I needed anything, no problem. Did we want to drive their brand-new Mercedes? No problem, because a car was a car and a family was family. So, I had a hard time getting it. I mean there are insurance and rentals if something were to happen.

Even though I was immediately resistant at first, thinking only of me, I came to an understanding of where she was. She had just lost her dad and husband and had to re-learn how to live her life as a single, independent woman. Her car symbolized something precious to her that she wasn't willing to risk losing just yet. She grew up in a state of lack. It is not my place to judge whether she still lives there to this day. I have to accept and have compassion for the path she is on and love her unconditionally. After all, I chose this woman to be my Mother. And really, I didn't "need" her car. I had other options. Perhaps, had I not had other options, the situation would have played out differently. However, there was a lesson in there for me. And maybe there was a lesson in there for her.

I ended up going to that show driving my dad's truck, which he so generously lent me for over a month as I stayed in Indiana to begin this book and have time to myself.

We can't *make* people see things, events, or circumstances the way we see them. We can't make people do the things we'd do. We have to love and accept everyone in the most non-judgmental, compassionate way we can. I had to learn that again at that moment. I have to learn this over and over still when it comes to others. My Mother grew up with little. Family members physically and emotionally abused her. She had a dad who abandoned her entire, five-kid family, and then she stayed in an unhappy marriage because

"God" wanted her to for years. I can only imagine that there are some serious things she is working out, and this is just one place she is in right now. And it too shall pass.

These are the kind of situations you're going to come across in life, in a million different scenarios. And this car business isn't even a big deal. I appreciate the lesson at the moment for me to understand that her opinions and the way she sees things aren't right or wrong, nor are they for me to fix or judge. So, when little OR big stuff like that tests you, take that opportunity to thank God, the Universe, for giving you the chance to look beyond what you want in your mind and practice compassion for someone else.

Suggestions:

1. Notice any situation that arises today that may cause you to get upset or offended. Rather than giving in to those feelings, take the higher road by being compassionate.

2. Remember that we are all one. Make an effort to see YOURSELF in the other person.

3. Don't forget to show yourself some compassion too. It helps to practice compassion with you because it makes it easier to show

compassion for others. Remind yourself that connecting with your Source makes the rest of this life and compassion business flow the way it needs to flow.

30. Fuck Your Buts and Your "Imma Try"

This chapter kind of goes back to the whole, "Fuck your excuses" line I said in the Introduction. If you want to have a fulfilling, magical life of kickassdom, stop saying you're going to "try", and for fuck's sake, please stop using the word "but" after talking about what you'd like to do in this time/space continuum we're in and do it already.

I have this thing when people say they're going to "try" to do something. And I also have an aversion to people saying, "I would love to do this or that, but..." These are big red flags and big fat excuses.

When the word "try" is used, it pretty much says to me that it went in one ear and out the other. "I'll try to make it." "I'll try to stick with it." "I'll try to get it done." Guess what? You won't make it, stick with it, or get it done because trying and doing are lifetimes apart. It's high time to change the language and words we use. A better alternative could be, "I intend to," unless, of course, you don't intend to. At least you're honest. However, if you change the language, "intending to do something" is way bigger than trying to do something.

As far as saying "but" goes, look, I get it. Life has gotten to you. Perhaps you veered off course, and you're not in the place you thought you'd be when those big dreams you were dreaming got eaten up and swallowed. Well, guess what? I'M in your corner. I want you to understand that you can create EVERYTHING you want. You are 10,000% capable of living your dreams. It's not the life that gets in the way of not living a life you love ...it's YOU and your excuses. It's IMPERATIVE to understand the power of YOU.

Why are you settling for a life of mediocrity? And at what point will you stop settling? Those are two very serious questions I'd like you to contemplate. And then write down the answers.

I was hanging out with a friend recently, who happens to be a gifted musician and has some pretty big dreams. "But," and there's that damn word, he continuously makes excuses as to why he can't do what he wants to do. Honestly, he can. When you choose to focus on how-to, rather than why you can't, you'll have a clearer picture in your head, and you'll be able to get unstuck from where you currently are.

If you think about it, doing what you love is natural. Doing what you love shouldn't be hard. If you're in alignment with your Source, living the life of your dreams is taking the path of least resistance, because Source knows nothing of failure. Sure, there may be some outside struggles. You may get told "no." But you don't give up. If I had given up after the first 20 "no's" I got about this book, you wouldn't be reading this. Look, if you're going to have resistance, please don't let that resistance come from yourself.

Furthermore, when you make a promise, the promise shows you have an intention. When you follow through with a commitment, it shows that you have good character. Granted, people make promises every day, and circumstances certainly change, i.e., divorce, unforeseen changes in people, kid obligations, work stuff, life stuff. But be fucking honest. If you don't want to do something, it's a lot easier just to let someone know you're not into it. Or at least make up some excuse, but don't fucking say, "I'll try."

Bottom line is this…things that come up in life; if it aligns with your spirit, say "yes," and if it doesn't – say "no". The word "try" is a scapegoat, period. You know it. I know it. Be who you are. If you don't want to go somewhere that someone asks you to or be a part of an event that someone asks you to be a part of, please don't say you'll "try" to make it. If you legit WANT to make it, but may not be able to out of prior obligations, then state that. "I would like to make that, but I may not be able to." Or say, "I intend" on something. Be intentional in everything you do in life.

Suggestions:

1. Remove "try" from your vocabulary for a while and see what

happens.

2. Live with intention every day. Do what you say you're going to do, and don't say you're going to do things that you don't want to do. Just be who you are and do the things you love.

3. Fuck your excuses. Please get out of excuse mentality. Remove doubt, fear, and worry from your mind. Then remove the words, "I'm not sure," "I can't," and "but" from your vocabulary. You can be sure when you are in pure alignment with the all- creating Source, and you can do all things with this Source. So, fuck your "butts" and your "try's."

31. Travel as Much as You Can

"It is better to travel well than to arrive." - Buddha

If there is an opportunity to travel, do it. We live in this vast world full of beauty, mystery, different cultures, fantastic food, but lessons ALL around. I can't tell you the number of beautiful souls I've met traveling. And the lifelong lessons that I've learned, one being, "I control NOTHING, so be fucking cool all the time and go with the flow."

Accurate reality checks happen when you travel. You can also learn a hell of a lot about someone when you travel with them. Legit, there are people I will never travel with again, and most likely won't even be friends with because it's not worth the hassle of hearing someone bitch about idiotic things. You learn the real character of yourself and others when you go for a ride.

I've been fortunate to be able to go on so many fun adventures; such as traveling to exotic places, zip-lining through forests, wave running through amazing oceans, sleeping on beaches, and touring in a van across the United States with a band. Traveling is so inspiring to me. I love living on the road. I even took a road trip to Chicago to clear my head while doing this book, to observe and keep on a creative path.

Whenever an opportunity presents itself to you to visit someplace new, jump on it full force. Traveling is an opportunity for you to learn about other cultures while letting your beautiful, soul light shine. The world we live in is so beautiful, so enjoy it.

Also, whenever you get the opportunity to meet new people at a party, dinner, or outing, please do it. You never know who is going to come into your life to help you on your way. The Universe has perfect timing, and you never know when your time is about to come, so be as open as you can to impact as many people as you can with your unfuckwithable badass self.

Suggestions:

1. Getaway, even if it's close to your home. Find a state park, a hiking trail, anything to get out in nature. Take some time and save up some money, a little bit at a time, and go on that trip you've been dying to go on. When you put the idea in your head, start taking the necessary steps to get there.

2. If you don't have a passport, get one, especially if you plan on traveling overseas or in different countries. This advice is travel 101. Don't "wait" until you have the trip booked. By taking action now,

you're letting the Universe know you're ready and serious about getting out and about.

3. Love every second of it. If there are delays, love them. They may be saving you from something that may not have been in your best interest. If there are hiccups, look for a new opportunity to be in a different state of mind. Love, learn, and please respect the different cultures in this big, beautiful world of ours. Traveling is one of the best ways to learn about yourself, other cultures, and the true beauty and abundance of the world we live in.

32. The Left Lane Is for PASSING – So, Please, Get the Fuck Over

Oh, and while you're traveling and out there, let's talk about something else that can be changed: Being considerate of others when you drive. It's so annoying when people drive slow in the passing lane. I like to call these people "regulators" and not in a good sense of the word. You know, when you're on a highway and there's a passing lane, but the person in the passing lane is driving the same speed as the person in the cruising lane. It's like they're regulating traffic. Please get the fuck over. It's especially annoying when they're doing it with a phone in their hands.

The point here: Be considerate of other people.

No suggestions needed here. You get the point.

Lindsay Manfredi

33. Marriage Should Never Be Your End Destination

This may be coming out of left field, but I have something to say about marriage. I've been married once. I'm not sure if I ever will be again. That's where I am right now. Who knows, the right person and circumstance could come along and change my mind. I'm open. However, looking back, as it's been fourteen years since I said my first "I do" and eleven years since I ate those words, I realized I got married for all the wrong reasons, as many people do. While there is nothing wrong with marriage, please, please, PLEASE understand what you're in for before you hastily make that decision.

Relationships take a lot of work. Unless your relationship with yourself is top-notch, all your other relationships will suffer. There will be too many expectations, too many disappointments, and your marriage will most likely fail. According to the Bureau of Labor Statistics, approximately forty-two percent of marriages that took place between ages fifteen and forty-six ended in divorce by age forty-six. Women were more likely to marry and remarry than were men. Also, marriages of women were more likely to end in divorce, as were marriages that began at younger ages. On average, women married younger than men.

These numbers make me wonder what that says about us. My marriage failed due to several reasons. One was that I didn't know

WHO I was or how I was going to grow. I always knew I wanted to make music, but at that time, I didn't think I could. I was thinking small, 1 and was settling for a person versus pursuing my dreams. However, he was the one who eventually helped me realize more of my dreams. It also failed due to a lack of respect and communication, which ultimately led to anger and resentment. It was toxic, so we had to walk away. Additionally, I imagined I would gain "security" if I got married. I also thought I had a trophy husband and wanted to tie that shit down. Reality check, people STILL look at other people whether they're married or not.

I jumped in headfirst, not even knowing who I was marrying. He was nearly two decades older than me. I had no right to get married in the amount of time I did, which was within six months of us getting together. Once again, getting married for security reasons, whether you're insecure with yourself or you think it's something you're "supposed" to do because of social or family expectations, are fucked up reasons to get married.

In an interview on *Loose Women*, beloved actress Goldie Hawn said that the reason her relationship with actor Kurt Russell has lasted so long is that they've never walked down the aisle. She said they would have divorced if they had been married. She expressed that she chose to stay, and he decided to stay, and they were both happy with that decision. Hawn said, "There is something psychological about not getting married because it gives you the freedom to make decisions one way or the other." Her main point; it's essential to not lose yourself in the other person, which is something I've struggled with in the past, along with many people I know.

I'm not saying by any means that you shouldn't get married. Hell, if the right person comes along for me, I may go for it. What I AM suggesting is to question your motives. Know WHO YOU are, along with who your partner is before getting into something even harder (and way more expensive) to get out of.

I'm a firm believer that everything happens for a reason. I learned SO much from my ex-husband, and I'm extremely grateful that he encouraged me to pick up a bass. We had great times, we had terrible times, and I don't regret any of it. It was all a learning process to guide me into being the person I am today. A couple of serious boyfriends since then have also taught me lessons. And I'm still fucking growing.

While I have no plans to get married now, if I ever do again, it will be because I want to, because I am genuinely in love, not for some bogus reason.

Don't be tied down to shit that's going to tie you down. Take TIME with a huge life decision like that. Do it for the RIGHT reasons if you're going to do it at all. Marriage doesn't save relationships, and neither do babies.

Suggestions

1. Please, please, please get to know, love, and respect the shit out of yourself. Love yourself as hard as you can and then love others. Do not settle for anything less than what you want. Make a list of traits you want in a future spouse, and don't veer from what speaks truth to you. You deserve to be loved and respected and honored. Once you are that much in love with yourself, you will expect nothing less. And you're full inside whether you're with someone or not because that's how you roll.

2. Forgive any of your past "perceived" mistakes you've made. You were where you needed to be at the time. Don't judge yourself because Source never judges you. It only loves.

3. Take your time. Always remember that anything meant for you WILL NOT pass you by, so there's genuinely no need to rush.

34. We All Want to Be Loved - So BE Love

I have a very important vision for this book. My bigger end goal is to start a foundation where we can help change the social landscape with our middle school children. I will also write a book for kids to teach them to stop being little assholes. That will be a result of talking to adults in this particular version of helping others live in their creative power.

On November 4, 2016, NBC News reported that suicide kills more middle school students than car crashes: "The suicide rate among U.S. middle school students doubled from 2007 to 2014, surpassing for the first time the incidence of youngsters who died in car crashes, federal researchers found."

In aggregate numbers, 425 young people ten to fourteen years of age took their own lives in 2014, compared with 384 who perished in automobile accidents that year, according to the CDC.

What the FUCK is going on? I've read enough articles and seen enough *Dr. Phil* previews to know in my heart that bullying, social media, and cyberbullying most likely have something to do with this increase. The bottom line; we aren't teaching our children to be lovers, and that shit starts in the home. If you have kids that bully in any way, you're not doing your job. It has nothing to do with "laying down the law," but everything to do with your behavior daily.

Being the mother of a child in this age range, I couldn't possibly imagine someone hurting her or bullying her. I also couldn't believe her bullying someone else. I remember being bullied in high school back in the late 90s. Bitches were mean. Someone always had something to prove. And if those people who bullied me are anything like their bully parents (God, it's so cliche), then we can see how this cycle of bullshit continues. We have to make it stop. This is why you must fill your cup first. This is why we must TALK WITH your children and not TO them. We must teach tolerance and love. We are not all the same, and that's the most beautiful thing. We have to show love by BEING love. We have to teach tolerance by being understanding and tolerant. We have to teach patience by being patient.

You can't fight racism with racism. You can't fight hate with more hate. You can't fight a war with more bombs. We, as a human race, one blood, have to change the way we think and the way we respond to things. We need to stop "fighting," and start loving. Future generations depend on it. We also have to keep in mind that we can't give away what we don't have. So we must learn to LOVE ourselves so that we can share the love with others.

In Dr. Wayne Dyer's book, *10 Secrets for Success & Inner Peace,* he describes this perfectly:

You can only give away what you DO have, and all that you're giving away every day are items from your inventory. If you give away hatred, it's because you've stored up hatred inside of you to give away. If you give away misery, it's because you have a ready supply available from which to select and distribute.

Dr. Dyer describes how we absolutely MUST learn to love ourselves to give love to others. We must be kind to ourselves to be kind to others. We must forgive ourselves to show forgiveness, and so on. How we treat ourselves and how our young people see us, ALL has a significant impact on their behavior.

We shouldn't try to mold our children into the perfect version of them that we see FOR THEM. The exact opposite should be taking place. We have to let them know it's okay to be who they are, especially when they don't know who the hell they are. Most of us adults have the same struggle. I'm going to give an example from my time at Girls Rock! Indianapolis.

All of the volunteers, including the other co-founders who would spend a week at camp, would continuously say, "Man, I wish I would have had something like this when I was a kid." We're not trying to hold hands, kumbaya, give trophies to everyone, or any of that bullshit. We were simply talking about a *support* system that mattered and still does. We're talking about a place where no one is judged for who they're morphing into as humans. Granted, we all turned out okay, but we're adults. Today's landscape is much more grey, and we have to support our children by loving them, accepting them, and helping them, just as you want to be loved, accepted and supported.

Suggestions:

1. Just as we want to feel love, we must give love. Perhaps an answer for you would be to volunteer to be a Big Brother or Big Sister or look into your local rock camps. Think about something that you can offer to help mold a young person's life.

2. Start to recognize yourself in everyone you come across. We ALL, as a human race, come from the same Source. "We are all brothers and sisters in the end," to quote Band of Skulls. Take away religion, race, and sex...all of it. When we're stripped out of our physical beings, our Spirits will be reunited in a flurry of love and observation. We are all expanding, so while we're here, let's expand to tolerant, loving, peaceful humans. It begins right inside your own heart.

3. Look inward and notice your thoughts and how they reflect on

your behavior. Transform any negatives to love as much as you can. Radiate THAT, and you're making a difference in the lives of so many.

35. No More Lies

There are times when I'm not happy. I'm not going to pretend to be. There are times I'm at my highest-vibing self. There are times I let my emotions get the best of me. The struggle is a real-life thing. Right now, in this particular moment, writing this specific section, I'm feeling a little lost. I'm a little pissed off, and I'm even a little scared. In life, we take the good with the bad and do our best to switch things around as they need. That's the beautiful power of choice. We may say life's not always going to be rainbows, sunshine, and fucking unicorns. Or we may say, it's not always going to be easy. If that's what you want to believe, then you're right. It won't be easy. Or you can recognize what's going on inside you and turn your story around. No one is going to create our dream life for us.

I'm going to go out on a limb here and assume you don't want people to lie to you. How many of you know someone you'd like to be honest with, but aren't sure you want to put yourself out there like that? You may be concerned with not wanting to hurt their feelings, or you may not want to "rock the boat." If you're anything like me, you'll recognize this. I'm not a fan of conflict at all, so I tend just to shut down and use avoidance tactics when faced with something I don't want to deal with in my life, which isn't always the best thing. It's an everyday thing I work on.

I know that I want honest, loving people in my life. If I have some bullshit, I'm happy to be called out on it. I need honesty in my life. I need trust. By that same token, I will not take or be responsible for hateful projections of other people onto me. All of us must know who we are for us to get to a point where we can decipher the difference between our shit and other people gaslighting us.

People who love you should strive to make you feel good. There are ways to give constructive criticism. If someone we love is making us feel bad, or is always on us, or lies to us, it's time to take the balls to reassess your relationship with that person. The issues you have with another person stem from you, no matter how much you'd like to place blame. The blame game is easy, a scapegoat, but it's bullshit. You and I are getting precisely what we asked for in life because good or bad, that's what's showing up.

I understand it can be hard to conceive that if we are dealing with a difficult situation in our life, that we attracted it, but that's merely 1000% true. Whatever vibration you are feeling, that is what's going to show up until your feelings and vibrations change. Universal law cannot be changed or manipulated. You can believe in it and make changes, or you can choose not to accept it and keep riding that struggle bus. I may get on it sometimes, but I'll be the first to find a stop as soon as I stop playing the victim role. I want you all to get off that bus and play the leading role in creating the perfect life for you. The keyword here is YOU. Not the ideal life for the people who are currently IN your life.

NEVER forget that you create your Universe. No one else can do it for you. The entire point of this book is to encourage you to get you to know yourself so well, that outside opinions that are going against your thoughts and beliefs mean nothing to you. My goal is for you to love yourself so much that none of that shit matters. My goal is for you to be so in tune with yourself and your Spirit that you are genuinely unfuckwithable.

It's time to stop lying to ourselves and others, get fucking real, and be honest fucking people. If you lie to other people or me to match an "image" you want to portray, you can fuck right off. If you want to lie to yourself, then do it. But as I said, you can't deny Universal law, The Law of Attraction. What do you want to attract in your life today?

Suggestions:

1. Take some time today and reflect on what's going on in your life. Do you like where you are, the people in your life, and how you feel? If you DO like what you see, good job. Keep doing what you're doing to continue loving every aspect of your life. If you don't, take

some notes. Whatever you do, BE HONEST about your feelings. Honor your feelings, but be aware of where they come from. Any feelings of hatred, blame, guilt, anger, or any bad feelings are not of Source.

2. When you begin to be aware of these feelings, you then have the power to change the conversation consciously. This will then give you the influence and ability to shift lower feeling vibrations to, hopefully, higher and more energetic GOOD vibrations, Marky Mark style.

3. Let go of the liars in your life, and this includes you. If you're hanging out with people you feel you need to "impress", so you make things more significant than they are or straight-up lie, then I'd encourage you to re-evaluate those folks. You don't need people like that in your new life, and you certainly can't thrive with people who are hanging on a level different than you, unless, of course, you'd like to stay where you are. But I think you don't, and I think you're better than that.

36. Life Is Fucking Magical

I'm about to wrap this bad boy up, but I can't until I share the story of how the Universe manifested all the things possible to the point where I'm playing in one of my all-time favorite bands, Cold. This co-creation story, which still blows me away, begins in 1998. I went to a concert at Deer Creek in Indianapolis, which is a big outdoor amphitheater. Multiple bands were playing that day. There was a particular band that was getting some attention called Sprung Monkey. They had a song called "Get Em Outta Here." I ended up meeting the guys, and their tour manager at the time and I hit it off. They were headed up to Chicago in a couple of days and asked me to help sell their merch because they didn't have anyone for the rest of the Midwest tour. However, they had the next night off in Indianapolis, so they invited me to join them to see Pearl Jam, playing at the same theater that following evening. So, being a huge Pearl Jam fan, I went with them.

The following night, I joined Sprung Monkey in Chicago for their show at the Metro opening up for the bands, Cold and Kid Rock. It was my first time hearing of the Jacksonville-based rock band. I immediately loved them. Their self-titled debut album was raw, honest, and intense, and I loved their singer, Scooter's, voice. They were everything I looked for in a band.

Before the show, we were all hanging out, so I got to meet the band, shoot the shit, and from that moment on, I was a fan. I was officially a part of the Cold Army. After the Chicago show, I went on with Sprung Monkey to Ohio, met some great folks, and then they were off to New York to play on Letterman. I went back home to Indiana and back to work.

At the time, I had just met my daughter's father, Jayme (I didn't have her until 2004), and was doing a body piercing apprenticeship at Tommy's Tattoos in Kokomo, Indiana, which is the city I grew up in. I wasn't playing as much music at the time, writing here and there, and WANTING to be a part of the music industry somehow. Time went on, and, after a year or so when I broke up with Jayme, I began writing more music. I moved to Terre Haute, IN, after meeting some super cool musicians who lived there, because they invited me to start a new project with them. So, I did it. I packed up my shit, my piercing portfolio, and started a new life.

I got a job at a great tattoo shop, got to work with the late, great tattooist, Bob Olson, and play in a band. I made so many friends, made enough money to support myself, go to shows, buy music gear, and have a pretty laid-back life. I loved it. But after a while, I knew I needed to get out of Terre Haute. It was a small college town, and nothing was happening musically there. There were more alcohol-fueled nights than anything productive.

However, it was a time of learning and fun. My bassist at the time and I decided to move to Gainesville, Florida, which promised a way better rock scene.

After living in Gainesville for a year or so, I decided to break all ties with my bassist. I'm still buddies with my guitarist, Ryan Mulroy though. While I had moved on from getting drunk every night, he had not. I had never really experienced what it was like to deal with someone who drinks ALL the time, so this was another foray into letting go of negative people in my life. I was learning early to let go and move on when shit wasn't right in my life. I had two choices: go home or choose a new place to move. I was unable to get a job working as a body piercer in Gainesville, where I was making minimum wage at a gas station, and I had no ties there. My most mature girlfriend, Cassandra, rest her soul, had moved to Pinellas Park in Florida, which is a part of Saint Petersburg. She had a little trailer, let me know I was a complete dumbass for even considering going back to Indiana, and told me to get down there. I mean, we shared a BED for a MONTH. Her generosity in housing me gave me the time to look for a piercing job in Tampa, get familiar with the music scene, and search for bands who needed a vocalist. I had a new job in Ybor City, my apartment in Tampa, and had placed ads to begin a new band within six weeks of moving there.

Talk about the Universe having my back. I was doing so

well and was so happy I eventually invited my best friend at the time to get her ass out of Indiana and come to Florida too. During that time, I was playing in a band I put together called Pretty Machine Gun and had my first actual studio recordings. We were playing shows, and I was making great money in the tattoo industry. Life was rad. And I couldn't have been happier.

Now, because I was the head piercer and manager of a tattoo shop, I was having some work issues because my band was scheduling shows for the weekends, and my tattoo shop was a high-volume shop. I needed an excellent, reliable piercer to help take on that hecticness. So, I phoned up my ex, Jayme, to see if he'd move down and help me out. He did.

During this time, Cold was releasing their second studio album, *13 Ways to Bleed Onstage*. Of course, I picked it up. I was so in love with this album that I got the spider, which is their trademark band logo, tattooed on my arm, so that when I was holding a microphone, I could always represent this band whose music meant so much to me. If you've ever read the book or seen the movie *The Secret*, my friend, Paul Lushin calls this act one of my "Secret" moments or my "Law of Attraction" moments.

The following year, Cold was working on their follow-up album *Year of the Spider,* and asked their fans to submit their Cold tattoos for the album. The photo my sister took of my tattoo made it, and it happened to be next to the bassist whom I replaced. That record went Gold, so there has been a photo of me on Scooter's wall since then. He had no idea that was me in the sleeve of the record.

My band had broken up in Tampa, and I was in love, so I needed to follow my heart. I left my job to move to Chicago to attempt, once again, a relationship with Jayme (still no baby at this time). When it didn't work out, I swallowed my pride, and decided to move back home and maybe, finally go to college. I ended up getting my personal trainer's license in the interim, while waiting to become a resident of Indiana again, and boom, on a random visit back from Jayme, we conceived Bella. We made another attempt or two at a good relationship. That just wasn't in the cards for us, so we co-parent, all of which I've talked about.

After living in Indiana for a little over a year, I was finally a resident, so I enrolled at IU Kokomo. This began my five-year journey into getting my degree. During this time, I ended up getting engaged, breaking off the engagement, and marrying someone else, which ultimately lead to me learning how to play bass. My ex-husband was, and still is, one of the best bassists I've ever seen. Had these steps not happened in my life, I have no idea where I would be today. My ex-husband was a great teacher for me in so many ways.

Learning to play the bass came naturally to me because I had been playing guitar for nearly a decade, with time off here and there.

I found that I loved the bass much more than the guitar. My husband and I started a band called We're Not Mexican, which was the first band I played bass in. I loved it. I loved the rockabilly type style of music we wrote and played, but after we divorced, that band broke up. I then joined Neon Love Life, then Kaleidostars, and then PictureYes. PictureYes toured with Saving Abel for a couple of months while I was a member.

On October 14, 2014, I was on my way to a gig when I got a tweet from the Cold Twitter account. It was the singer, Scooter, asking me to check my Facebook messages because he had sent me a message. I had a feeling but didn't know, but I was super excited nonetheless. He asked me to call him, gave me his number, and I called him immediately. That was it. The rest is history. I said yes without hesitation. Biggest honor of my life.

So, to hear Scooter tell the story of how he came across me, Facebook was the beginning. The band had been doing some fundraising for the LIVE DVD and album they were putting out for their fans. I had posted a shot of me playing my bass that showed the Cold spider. Someone saw it who knew they were looking for a bassist because their old bassist was joining another band. They sent Scooter the photo and said, "She's already branded. Let's check her out." So, they did. And they researched me, YouTubed me, saw what I was about. And decided I was the one they wanted to bring in. I am truly blessed, and I don't think it was a coincidence that brought this current group together. I worked hard, and I am still working and learning everything I need to know. I am still growing musically. I just had the best time of my life being able to record an album with one of my heroes and be on the road with my brothers. In addition, the hearts of my new bandmates are so on point. Everything is flowing naturally, and all of it feels good. No, it feels better than good. It feels amazing.

I know that everything in my past has led me to this point where I finally get to make a living doing what I love. I feel beyond full and beyond excited. Hard work pays off. I had the dream I've always had handed to me, but was it just handed to me? While it was, in a way, it's also been twenty-two years of preparation and never giving up that got me here.

I could have made different life choices along the way, but the Universe has had my back the entire time. I was able to tap into a Universal power when I began to be conscious of what I really wanted in life, and that started decades ago. I created my dream in the quantum force. A dream that consisted of me being on stage, having publishing checks direct deposited, of getting to meet other creative people in the industry and surrounding myself with greatness. I haven't made all the best choices in the world. I've done my fair share of partying and living hard. It's funny, the older I get, the healthier I want to live. But the time and experiences I've had, from my perceived failures to heartbreak, have made me into who I am today.

I know for a fact that if you work toward a dream or a goal, and you co-create that with the Universal power that you have inside of you, the Universe will take note. The Universe wants you to have everything you need, and all of your desires met. The Universe is so grand and so giving, but you'll reap the benefits of that relationship faster if you follow some of the advice I've just given you. Get in touch with your Source. Get in touch with your Spirit side because it will keep on going. There is no end to your spirit. You are immortal. You NEED to understand that. Live fearlessly. Live boldly. Live your dream. The more successful you are, the more you can give back to the human race. It's a beautiful circle if you rise above the bullshit you create in your own life. Ain't nobody got time for that lame shit.

Get out there and be better. DO better, but don't beat yourself up if you fall along the way. We all fucking fall. That's when we can reevaluate and get back on the right track. I believe in your beautiful, unfuckwithable soul. It's high time you did too.

Suggestions:

Un*fuck*withable

1. I love you. I believe in you. We are all brothers and sisters, and I think we can create a movement of love, peace, joy, and undeniable support for one another. My Facebook page for Unfuckwithable is up and going. Share your stories. Lift one another. Get on board with living in your Power.

2. To reiterate my belief in the notion that we are all one, I'm going to share with you the 52nd Verse of the Tao Te Ching:

All under heaven have a common beginning.
The beginning is the Mother of the world.
Having known the Mother,
we may proceed to know her children.
Having known her children,
we should go back and hold onto the Mother.

Keep your mouth shut,
guard the senses,
and life is ever full.
Open your mouth,
always be busy,
and life is beyond hope.

Seeing the small is called clarity;
keeping flexible is called strength.
Using the shining radiance
you return again to the light
and save yourself from misfortune.

This is called
the practice of eternal light.

3. Keep radiant. Keep vigilant. And please, friend, love as hard as you can.

About the Author

Photo Credit: Emily Tingley

Lindsay Manfredi is a renaissance woman who has pushed creative and spiritual boundaries throughout her life. Currently, she is the bassist for the multiple-gold-record-awarded, alternative rock band Cold. Manfredi previously rocked the Indianapolis social media and marketing scene for ten years with Linzstar Inc, featured prominently in speaking engagements from Blog Indiana to Bloomington's The Combine.

She has been published multiple times in various online media outlets, including Arianna Huffington's Thrive Global community. She co-founded Girls Rock! Indianapolis, a nonprofit rock and roll summer camp for girls ages 8-16, and has been a two-time TEDx speaker, spreading her experiences and encouragement to the community. Indianapolis Monthly Magazine named Manfredi, a top up-and-coming artist in 2013.

Manfredi has been touring in support of Cold's most recent album, *The Things We Can't Stop*, (Napalm Records, September 2019), all the while finishing her first book, *UNFUCKWITHABLE: A Guide to Inspired Badassery*. As a singer/songwriter, Manfredi is a frequent collaborator with Geno Lenardo (Filter, Chevelle), and has original music featured on the *Fitfluential Radio* podcast. She keeps her toe in the marketing world through particular popup projects, including limited luxury candle collections with Tricia Meteer of Equinox Farms and partnerships with Ernie Ball and Jim Dunlop. She has two signature series basses with Diamond Guitars.

Made in the USA
Middletown, DE
17 September 2021